WHEN THE FIRE FALLS

TEN CHARACTERISTICS OF GENUINE REVIVAL

TERRY LONG

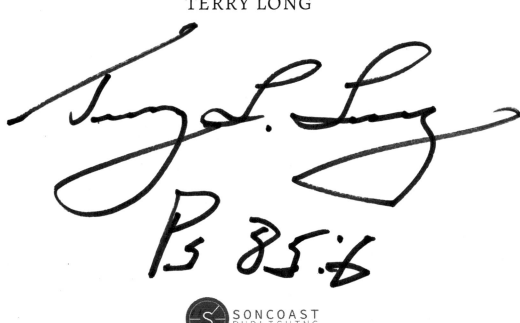

When the Fire Falls

Copyright ©2021 Terry Long

All rights reserved. This book or any portion thereof may not be reproduced or used in any manner without the express written permission of the publisher except for the use of brief quotations in a book review.

Scripture taken from the New King James Version®. Copyright © 1982 by Thomas Nelson. Used by permission. All rights reserved.

ISBN Paperback: 978-1-953406-32-3

ISBN ebook: 978-1-953406-33-0

Cover designed by Jesse Conte

Soncoast Publishing

PO Box 1503, Hartselle, AL 35640

www.soncoastpublishing.com

To my four children, LeAnn, Natalie, Terra, and Brett.

And my nine grandchildren, Walker, Anna Grace, Wesley, Caleb, Dani Lynn, Jacey, Bridges, Macy, and Marlee.

No father or grandfather could ask for a more beautiful legacy than what I have in you. You have enriched my life more than words can say, and I wish for each of you the fullest measure of happiness and love possible.

CONTENTS

Foreword	vii
Endorsements	ix

PART I
WHAT IS REVIVAL?   1

1. When the Fire Falls	3
2. What is This Thing We Call "Revival"?	15
3. Do We Really Need Revival?	25

PART II
TEN CHARACTERISTICS OF GENUINE
REVIVAL   37

4. Characteristic # 1 Repentance	39
5. Characteristic # 2 Brokenness	53
6. Characteristic # 3 Reconciliation	73
7. Characteristic # 4 Joy	91
8. Characteristic # 5 Lordship	105
9. Characteristic # 6 Prayer	135
10. Characteristic # 7 The Word	159
11. Characteristic # 8 Worship	171
12. Characteristic # 9 Soulwinning	183
13. Characteristic # 10 Awakening	205
About the Author	213
Also by Terry Long	215

FOREWORD

I remember it as a lazy summer Sunday evening in Frankfort, Kentucky. Life was good. We rode bikes in the neighborhood and played kickball until dark. However, something happened one summer evening at Buck Run Baptist Church that changed my life. Some months earlier in 1970, fire fell at Asbury College, a small Methodist school around thirty miles from Frankfort. What started as an "ordinary" chapel service shook the entire campus. In reality, this chapel was anything but ordinary. Night and day, for over a week, the chapel service continued without a break. Classes were canceled. Lives were changed. The Holy Spirit touched students, professors, and visitors. But this revival fire didn't stop in that little town of Wilmore, Kentucky. Students began to travel and share what God was doing. Everywhere they went, it was like a fire striking dry brush; revival would break out. This revival spread to over 130 campuses and multiple countries.

On this particular evening, I entered the church where students, touched and inspired by the Asbury Revival, led the service. I don't remember anything these young people said. All I know is that fire came! I began to weep. I realized the depth of my sinfulness (as much as a young boy can understand) and the glory of Christ's salvation. Like Christian in *The Pilgrim's Progress*, I left my burden at the cross. Jesus saved me, and nothing has ever been the same.

Tasting revival creates a yearning within me to experience another outpouring of God's Spirit. In fact, I am praying for an even greater move of God! Our country needs Christ. The norm is immorality, lawlessness, lack of respect for authority, division, hatred, crime, pride, and millions of other vices. Remember, Christ can change all this in a moment. I sense fresh winds of the Spirit blowing across our land. Christians are praying. There is a renewed sense of urgency and expectancy in the Church. Could another spiritual awakening be right around the corner?

God raised up Dr. Terry Long for such a time as this! A long-time practitioner and student of revival, he has written *When the Fire Falls* to examine ten characteristics of genuine revival. His prayer is that God will use this book to rouse Christians to the reality of the power of God. He longs for God to send another great awakening! I am convinced God inspired Terry to pen these words. As you read his book, pray that God will drive our country to its knees. Furthermore, ask Him to set you ablaze by His Spirit. May we all pray, *Lord, send a great revival and let it begin with me*!

~Rob Jackson, Ph.D.
Alabama Baptist State Board of Missions
Director of Church Health and Spiritual Renewal

ENDORSEMENTS

Out of gimmicks and facing steady moral decline, the Church finds its back against the wall and in desperate need of a fresh wind from heaven that brings a restoration of the fullness and power of the Holy Spirit. If you hear the spiritual alarm bells ringing, and your own heart yearns for revival, then "When the Fire Falls: Ten Characteristics of Revival" will encourage, motivate, and inspire you in your quest. Terry Long has drawn from history, great prophetic voices of the past and his own experience of the work of Spirit in his life to bring to us a book for the hour. Find your place on the battlefield of prayer and let's "pray up" until God rends the heavens and comes in power to heal and restore the Bride of Christ.

~Dr Gordon Fort, Senior Ambassador to the President
International Mission Board

I've read up to chapter 8. Brother, the Fire has fallen on you! That room must have been ablaze with the Glory as you wrote what was busting from your heart to the page! This is Hallelujah work, my friend! Love it! Authentic. Pithy. These are not embers. No, these are coals aflame! Thanks for sharing. I'll finish this by tomorrow and

ENDORSEMENTS

start reading it again. Loved the cutting edge teaching, admonition, and challenge! I agree with the black church folk...there's a whooping in your soul and in this book. Preach on! Write on!

~Bob Weber, Senior Pastor
Valley Creek Baptist Church,
Hueytown, AL

In the days that we live in, it is unusual to begin a book that immediately speaks to the heart. Terry Long has been with God and this volume accomplishes this. The work is so personal that it captures, convicts, and challenges from the very beginning. As the book flows, there is a steady prompting for self-examination as the question confronts the reader, "How desperate am I for revival?" To read the accounts of how God moved in days past ignites a burning desire to cry out for a sweeping movement today. Always, as Terry writes, the focus and subject is on Jesus, all in all. This book has had a strong impact on my life and I pray that it will affect every believer deeply.

~Ken Jenkins,
Heavens Eyes Ministry/Illustrated Principles
Gatlinburg, TN

Drawing from an impressive compilation of history, theology, and reasoned supposition, Dr. Terry Long gives the Christian church a needed guide for understanding spiritual revival. This is a must read for every serious Christ follower who desires to see a genuine spiritual movement in the modern age.

~Dr. Matthew Burford, Apologetics Strategist
Alabama Baptist State Board of Missions

My mentor, friend, and brother in Christ, Terry Long has written this book on revival. I have known Terry Long for 30 years. This book is an inspiration to all who read it. I have seen revival in his

ENDORSEMENTS

ministry many times through the years. His dependence on Almighty God and his personal relationship with our Savior Jesus Christ resonates from his countenance. His confidence and trust in the Holy Spirit is evident in all that he says and does. I strongly recommend this book to all who are looking for genuine revival in their church as well as their own personal relationship with the Master and Savior Jesus.

~Richard Louviere, Pastor
Woodlawn Baptist Church in Iowa, LA.

Dr. Terry Long has hit the center of the bullseye concerning the current need for true revival. The heart of Dr. Long is revealed as he so wonderfully reaches back in time to review the history of revival, and then brings that truth into the current need for a true God sent revival for our day in which we live. The desperation of his heart is anchored in the centerpiece of true revival "the cross upon which Christ died for the sins of the whole world." This book is a must read for the person who is seeking a fresh move of God in their life.

~Dr. Jacky Connell, Senior Pastor
Eden Westside Baptist Church, Pell City, AL

I

WHAT IS REVIVAL?

Revive Us Again

"We praise Thee, O God!
For the Son of Thy love;
For Jesus Who died
And is now gone above
Hallelujah! Thine the glory
Hallelujah! Amen
Hallelujah! Thine the glory
Revive us, again.

All glory and praise
To the Lamb that was slain
Who has taken our sins
And has cleansed every stain

Hallelujah! Thine the glory
Hallelujah! Amen.
Hallelujah! Thine the glory
Revive us again.

Revive us again
Fill each heart with Thy love
May each soul be rekindled
With fire from above

Hallelujah! Thine the glory
Hallelujah! Amen
Hallelujah! Thine the glory
Revive us again

1

WHEN THE FIRE FALLS

"Once you've experienced the fire, you can never be satisfied with the smoke"
--Statement from the Welsh Revival

It was the wee hours of the morning before it finally happened. In a barn, of all places. On a tiny island off the Northwest Coast of Scotland. The year was 1949, and in an old hay barn just outside the village of Barvas, a miracle was in the making unlike anything anyone had ever seen on the island of Lewis, or on any other island in the Hebrides for that matter.

In dramatic fashion, with astonishing results, God was about to answer the desperate prayers of a handful of church members who had been faithfully meeting in that barn for weeks pleading with God for revival to come to their village and their church. At 3:00 am their prayers were answered.

Night after night, hour after hour, and week after week, this tiny little band of praying men and women had met in the old barn on the outskirts of town from 10 pm to 3 am and bombarded heaven with their urgent pleas for an outpouring of the Spirit of God in genuine revival. They were deeply concerned. Their churches were dead, no one was being saved, baptisms had become a thing of the past, and legalism had wrapped its icy fingers around the necks of the churches and choked the very life out of them, resulting in a coldness in worship and a sharp decline in attendance. Noticeably absent from their services were the young people. They wanted nothing to do with the Church.

On this particular night in mid-December, after hours of praying and weeping before God, one of the young men, a deacon in the church, stood up and said in typical British idiom, *"Men, this is rubbish! It seems to me to be so much humbug to be praying as we are praying, to be waiting as we are waiting, if we ourselves are not rightly related to God. Could it be that we, the ones most concerned for a spiritual awakening, are the very ones standing in its way?"*

He then read from Psalm 24:3-5:

> *"Who shall ascend into the hill of the Lord? Or who shall stand in his holy place? He that hath clean hands, and a pure heart; Who has not lifted up his soul to an idol, Nor sworn deceitfully. He shall receive the blessing from the Lord, And righteousness from the God of His salvation."*

Closing his Bible, this young man lifted up his arms to Heaven, and cried out, *"God, are my hands clean? Is my heart pure?"*

And that's the moment it happened. Like a blanket, the Spirit of God fell on those in the barn and they suddenly found themselves prostrate before God on the floor, cut to the heart with deep conviction, and weeping uncontrollably as they poured out their sins to God in heartfelt confession and humble repentance.

Just before daylight, this humble group of intercessors, their cheeks still warm from the tears of that fresh encounter with God, left the barn and began walking back into the village. To their amazement, they discovered that at the very same hour the Spirit had fallen upon them in the barn, that same spirit of conviction had fallen on nearly everyone in the village, awakening them from their sleep and deeply convicting each one of their lostness. They had dressed and gone out into the streets and were kneeling along the roads, crying out to God for mercy and for salvation. Every home had lights on in it. No one could sleep because the awareness of God was so overwhelming!

Many had gathered at the police station of all places. "Why there?" you ask, "and not the church?" Two reasons. First, the village church was spiritually dead and it was widely known that the constable at the police station was a very godly man. And, second, right next door to the police station was the home of two elderly sisters by the names of Peggy and Christine Smith.

Peggy and Christine Smith were prayer warriors who were deeply burdened for revival. Peggy was 84 years old and completely blind. Christine was 82 and bent over with arthritis. Yet these two sisters felt God had given them a promise that He was going to visit the islands with revival. That promise was Isaiah 44:3, where God says *"I will pour water on the thirsty land, and streams on the dry ground."* In spite of their age and physical limitations, these two sisters laid hold of the throne of God and claimed that promise of God for Revival in their Barvas village church. Before dawn broke that day, it is said that most of the town was converted.

They had begun praying in their small cottage two to three nights a week from 10 pm to 3 am asking God to send revival. After several weeks of praying like this, Peggy had a vision of her church being full of young people and an unknown minister preaching from the pulpit.

Peggy sent for their minister, Rev. James Murray MacKay, and told him that the sisters sensed God was about to break through in revival and that he should get the church leaders together and pray at the same time they were praying in their cottage. This is what led the small band of prayer warriors to begin gathering in the barn on the outskirts of the village several nights a week. On the night the Spirit fell, hundreds were converted, revival began to spread to all the islands, and in the next five weeks 20,000 people came to a saving knowledge of Jesus Christ! Duncan Campbell, who was the minister Peggy Smith saw in her vision, came to preach and said that 75% of those converted in the Hebrides Revival were saved before they ever came to church!

An intense hunger for the Word of God enveloped the Islands of Lewis, Harris, Berneray, Tiree, and North Uist. The Bible was no longer read out of a sense of duty or tradition; it came alive. Old debts were paid. Bars were emptied. Several police stations and courts shut down for lack of crime and cases to try. Many preachers and missionaries received their calling to ministry. It was said that the presence of the Lord was so strong it would make your hair stand on end, and there was nowhere you could go to escape the palpable sense of the presence of the Lord. Many had a difficult time sleeping because of the extraordinary presence of the Holy Spirit. Day and night, whenever they awoke in the morning, or in the middle of the night, the presence of the Lord was there. The churches that had previously been empty and dead were packed out. The church in Barvas that seated 800 was full Sunday after Sunday.

And what about the young people? By the droves, they came from everywhere. On the night Duncan Campbell arrived in town, he was notified that a large number of young people had gathered at the church at 11 pm. It seems that 100 or more of these youth were at a dance hall in town when right in the middle of a dance the Spirit of God had fallen upon them. Not coincidentally, it was the exact hour that a godly young deacon was praying in the aisle of the church for the Spirit to fall upon the people of the town. Suddenly the music at this dance hall stopped, and the young people, who were overcome by conviction of sin, fled the dance hall like they were fleeing the plague, and made their way to the church house.

At exactly the same time, there were hundreds more young people who had already been in bed, but simultaneously, without any explanation, got out of bed, dressed themselves, and went running to the church. By the time Duncan Campbell got there, the Barvas church seating 800 was packed, people had begun singing Psalms, and many were in the aisles and in the pews on their knees, crying out to God to have mercy! The meeting continued until 4 in the morning and many were saved. God had heard the desperate prayers of his people, and on this tiny island 40 miles off the coast of Scotland, He had sent a mighty, earth-shaking revival!

This mighty moving of the Holy Spirit has become known as the Hebrides Revival, or the Hebridean Revival, or the Revival on the Island of Lewis. Whatever you call it, I can tell you that when I read stories like that of God pouring out His Spirit in genuine revival and spiritual awakening, something within me wants to cry out, "Do it again, Lord! Do it again!"

Can there be any question that the greatest need in America today is for a genuine, Christ-honoring, heaven-sent revival? Our nation is in turmoil. The Covid-19 pandemic has taken a horrendous toll not only on our families, our businesses, and our churches, but also on our peace of mind. In this last year and a half we have witnessed chaos, turmoil, and political upheaval beyond anything we have ever experienced before. Our nation seems hopelessly divided, leading many to wonder, "Is there really any hope for America, and for the kinds of changes we so desperately need?"

The answer to that question is an emphatic YES! I wouldn't be writing this book if I didn't believe that. Yes, it is getting increasingly dark outside. But as Adrian Rogers used to say, "It is growing spiritually dark outside. Gloriously dark!"

Many of the great revivals in history have come in a time of political upheaval and spiritual darkness similar to what we are experiencing right now. In fact, the most often quoted passage on revival is 2 Chronicles 7:14 which says,

> "...if my people, which are called by my name, shall humble themselves, and pray, and seek my face, and turn from their wicked ways, then I will hear from Heaven, and will forgive their sin and heal their land."

This may very well be the greatest verse on revival in the Bible! But the thing we often fail to realize is that the part we love to quote is only half of the verse. That's why it doesn't start with a capital "I" in the word "if." It is the second half of a sentence, and it is high-time we read the first half of the sentence! It says,

> *"When I shut up heaven and there is no rain, or command the locusts to devour the land, or send pestilence among my people, if My people who are called by My name will humble themselves, and pray, and seek My face, and turn from their wicked ways, then will I hear from heaven, and will forgive their sin and heal their land."*

Does it surprise you to know that the greatest revival verse in the Bible is sandwiched right in the middle of a sentence that is talking about God shutting up the heavens, withholding rain, allowing the locusts to devour the land, and sending pestilence among His people? Does that sound vaguely familiar to you? When you read the word "Pestilence" does Covid-19 come to mind, by any chance? You may ask, "But why would God do that?" The answer is in the very next verse: *"Now my eyes will be open and My ears attentive to prayer made in this place."* (v. 15)

God allows things like this to happen in order to get our attention and bring us to our knees in humility and repentance, so that we might return to Him and enjoy the blessings of his favor once again.

Inscribed on the Jefferson Memorial in Washington D.C. are these words spoken by Thomas Jefferson himself: *"Indeed, I tremble for my country when I reflect that God is just; that His justice cannot sleep forever."*

Dr. Erwin Lutzer, pastor of the Moody Memorial Church in Chicago, Illinois said, *"The God of the Bible will not endlessly tolerate idolatry and benign neglect. He graciously endures rejection and insults, but at some point, He might choose to bring a nation to its knees with severe discipline."*

I believe that is happening in our nation today. It's not that we need to repent and seek God for revival to avert the judgment of God. We are already under the judgment of God.

In a phone conversation just a few months ago with Claude King, the author of *Experiencing God, Fresh Encounter, Return to Me,* and numerous other works on revival, he made a comment that caught my attention. He said, *"God has given us so many warnings: 9/11, the 2008 Financial crisis, and now the Coronavirus. If we do not heed the warning this time, I don't know how many more chances God will give America."*

America is reeling not only from the division and turmoil of a divided nation, but from the devastating effects of the pandemic. It seems that God is trying to get our attention. He is the one who has allowed this to happen, and He is the only one who can heal us and deliver us from it.

I was reading in the book of Hosea one day and noticed these verses that seemed to speak to me about how we need to cry out to God:

> *"When Ephraim saw his sickness, and Judah saw his wound, then Ephraim went to Assyria and sent to King Jareb. Yet he cannot cure you, nor heal your wound. For I will be like a lion to Ephraim, and like a young lion to the house of Judah. I, even I, will tear them and go away; I will take them away, and no one shall rescue. I will return again to My place till they acknowledge their offense. Then they will seek My face; In their affliction they will earnestly seek Me."*

When Ephraim and Judah saw their sickness and their wound, instead of turning to God for their healing, they chose to put their trust in man (King Jareb). But God said that he (King Jareb) couldn't cure them of their illness, for it was caused by their sin and rebellion against God. God said that He, Himself was the cause of their problems, and He was waiting for them to acknowledge their offense and seek His face. It is God who is doing the speaking. Then in Chapter six, verses one through three, it is Hosea who speaks and this is what he says:

> *"Come, and let us return to the Lord; For He has torn, but He will heal us; He has stricken, but He will bind us up. After two days He will revive us; On*

the third day He will raise us up, that we may live in His sight. Let us know; Let us pursue the knowledge of the Lord."

That's what we must do. We must acknowledge our sinful ways and our rebellion to the ways of God and return to Him for healing and revival. That is what it will take for Him to have mercy on us, deliver us, not just from the pandemic, but from our own sinful ways, and allow us to experience genuine revival like they experienced on the Island of Lewis.

You see, the One who made us knows us. He knows what it will take to bring us to repentance. And He knows that it will often take pain. His judgments are not evil, but necessary and good, and we can turn to Him anywhere along the cycle of spiritual awakening. When God causes us pain, and when we see his judgments on our nation, we should rejoice that he loves us enough to do that which will bring us to repentance. God is speaking to us in our pain and we need to hear what He is saying! The brilliant writer, C.S. Lewis, once said, *"We can ignore even pleasure. But pain must be attended to. God whispers to us in our pleasures, speaks to us in our conscious, but He shouts to us in our pains; it is His megaphone to rouse a deaf world!"*

Those of us who have been around for a while know from experience the truth of that statement. We have learned that there are very few teachers in life that teach us more than a teacher named "Sorrow." Pain and suffering has a way of stretching us and growing us like nothing else. How many times have you heard it said that we grow spiritually more in the valleys of life than in the mountain top experiences? Remember the Folgers coffee commercial with Mrs. Olson? The unique thing about Folgers coffee according to Mrs. Olson was that it was "mountain grown." I used to say in some of my sermons that "the only thing that grows on the mountain top is Mrs. Olson's coffee; everything else grows in the valley!" In other words, although we all tend to relish those "mountain top" experiences, the truth is that it is in the valleys of life where we grow the most!

That's what Robert Browning Hamilton was alluding to when he poignantly wrote in his famous poem, "Along the Way":

> "I walked a mile with pleasure, she chattered all
>   the way;
> But left me none the wiser for all she had to say.
> But I walked a mile with Sorrow, and ne'er a word
>   said she;
> But oh, the things I learned from her, when Sorrow
>   walked with me!"

America is in a tough spot right now. We are definitely going through a valley. Fear, anxiety, anger, and confusion have gripped our nation and the church like a vise. What are we to do? Where do we turn for help? The Psalmist said,

> *"I will lift up my eyes to the hills; from whence comes my help? My help comes from the Lord, who made heaven and earth." (Psalm 121:1-2)*

It is time to cry out to God for Revival. Or, to use a new phrase I recently learned from reading Byron Paulus' groundbreaking book called *OneCry*, "It's time to cry up!" Have you ever heard of "crying up?" Until recently, I had never heard this phrase. But it makes perfect sense. Here's how Byron Paulus describes it:

It means to cry "up" to God, as opposed to crying out. Sometimes people cry out and their cries are born out of anger, or disappointment, or fear. Sometimes we cry at; sometimes we cry for; and sometimes we cry because. But crying up is a different kind of cry. It is a vertical cry. It is cry of desperation to the only one who can really help us.

~It's like the cry of Moses in Exodus 32, when God was about to destroy the people of Israel.

~It's like the cry of the Israelites in I Samuel 7:2 when they came together to grieve after the ark of the covenant had been stolen and the nation had lost the glory of God.

~It's like the cry of David in Psalm 85:6 when he looked to heaven with a broken heart and pleaded, "Wilt thou not revive us again, that thy people may rejoice in Thee!"

~Or when Isaiah the prophet cried with passion in Isaiah 64:1, "Oh! That you would rend the heavens; that you would come down!"

That's what crying up is like! And that's what we need to be doing if we expect to see our nation healed and revived by our great God.

Dr. Paulus shares five questions in his book that point us to this upward cry to God for revival. As I close this chapter, I would like to share these questions that have fueled my passion for revival:

> *1.* What if these really are the last days? *People have been saying this for years, but what if this really is the last days? What if they are right and the time is short? All indicators are pointing to the soon return of our Lord Jesus Christ. Based on a recent study of 2 Thessalonians 2, I am firmly convinced it is sooner than any of us think. What if the Coronavirus pandemic was God's last warning just before He comes? What if the riots in the streets that seemed to have reached a tipping point, are a fulfillment of "the falling away" (Greek; Apostasia, "rebellion") mentioned in 2 Thessalonians 2:3 as the one thing that must happen before Christ returns and the Antichrist is revealed?*
>
> *2.* What if America is not an exception to the judgment of God? *Yes, without a doubt we can say that we have been exceptionally blessed by God as a nation in our past, but that doesn't make America an exception to God's judgment for our sins. If we believe that we are somehow immune from reaping the consequences of our sins (think 55 million babies slaughtered through abortion) simply because we were established as a Christian nation, we are deceived and have bought into the devil's lie.*

3. What if the promises of God for revival are still true today? *God promised the nation of Israel that He would revive their hearts and heal their land if they would humble themselves, repent, and pray, and those same principles are repeated in the New Testament for our benefit. (James 4:8; Revelation 2-3)*

4. What if there really is "latter rain" in store for the earth as prophesied in the book of Joel? *This would refer to a sweeping move of the Holy Spirit resulting in a great harvest of souls just before the second coming of Christ.*

5. What if God is raising up a remnant of believers "for such a time as this?" *(And from what I can see, He is doing just that!)*

In 2011, in a conference on Revival & Spiritual Awakening at the Moody Bible Institute's Pastor's Conference, a visiting pastor from Uganda asked if he could share a comment and then ask a question. He was given permission to do so. He then told of the godly people of Uganda who had prayed for years for revival. God sent it in dramatic fashion, but it required devastation first. Their nation suffered horrible atrocities at the hand of a wicked government.

But eventually, the revival came. After experiencing the amazing results of revival, they then turned their prayers toward America. They began asking God to send an outpouring of His Spirit to our land, knowing that if America would experience genuine revival, it would impact the world. He said the leaders know that God will send revival…and that it will come either through desperation or devastation.

Then came the question. He asked, "*What are you Christian leaders in America doing to foster a spirit of desperation, so that it does not require devastation?*"

Good question. My friend, God is speaking. No question about it. He really is. But the crucial question is, "Are we listening?"

If we genuinely want revival like we say we do, then the question we need to be asking is, " Lord Jesus, what do You want to do in my life personally, that revival might come? What changes do *I personally* need to make in order for revival to come to my heart, my home, my church, and my community?

As the great evangelist Gypsy Smith used to say, *"If you want to have revival, get into your prayer closet, draw a circle on the floor with a piece of chalk, get inside the circle, and ask God to begin revival inside the circle. When He does, revival will be on."*

My friend, may I ask you a personal question? *Where is your chalk?*

Oh Lord! Will you pour Your Spirit out upon us once again and revive your people…beginning with me?

2

WHAT IS THIS THING WE CALL "REVIVAL"?

"God hath had it much on His heart, from all eternity, to glorify his dear and only-begotten Son; and there are some special seasons that he appoints to that end, wherein he comes forth with omnipotent power to fulfill his promise and oath to him. And these times are times of remarkable pouring out of his Spirit *to advance his kingdom; such a day is a day of his power…"*
--Jonathan Edwards

The term "revival" may be one of the most misunderstood terms in our Christian vocabulary. What exactly do we mean when we say something like, *"Hey! Come to our revival next week!"* or *"Boy! Do we ever need revival in this church!"* Or, *"How many did you have saved in your revival last week?"*

One of the dangers of our American brand of Christianity is that we often "contextualize" the Word of God. That is, we tend to hear God's Word in the context of our lives and current situations. This "cultural commentary" on the Word can sometimes alter our understanding of how Christianity is supposed to work. I'm afraid that we have done that with the concept of Revival. We have so "culturalized" and "contextualized" the idea of revival until we have unfortunately lost the meaning of the word altogether. So let's talk about what revival really is.

In his essay, "Jonathan Edwards and the Crucial importance of Revival," Dr. D. Martin Lloyd-Jones gives Edwards' definition of revival, which is "…a pouring out of His Spirit."Lloyd-Jones goes on to make the comment:

Today, we are hearing much about what is called "renewal." People dislike the term revival; they prefer renewal. What they mean by that is that we have all been baptized with the Spirit at the moment of regeneration, and that all we have to do, therefore, is to realize what we already have and yield ourselves to it. That is not revival! You can do all they teach and derive many benefits; but you still have not had revival. Revival is an outpouring of the Spirit. It is something that comes upon us; that happens to us. We are not the agents, we are just aware that something has happened. So Edwards reminds us of what revival is."

Revival is something outside ourselves. It is something that happens to us. We cannot do it ourselves. We cannot revive ourselves. Edwards tells us that revival is first and foremost a re-kindling of the fire within the heart of the believer; it is a pouring out of the Spirit of God upon God's people.

Correspondingly, it was the great preacher, G. Campbell Morgan who said, *"We cannot organize revival, but we can set our sails to catch the wind from heaven when God chooses to blow upon His people once again!"*

The songwriter, George Atkins, penned one of our oldest and most beloved American folk hymns in 1819, and the first verse echoes this truth that Revival is not something we can do for ourselves; rather is something that God sends upon us:

> "Brethren, we have met to worship
> And adore the Lord our God.
> Will you pray with all your power
> While we try to preach the Word.
> <u>All is vain unless the Spirit</u>
> <u>Of the Holy One comes down.</u>
> Brethren, pray and holy manna

Will be showered all around."

The hymn writer is saying that even though we meet for worship; even though we love and adore the Lord, our God; even though we pray and preach with all our power, nothing will happen unless "the Spirit of the Holy One comes down!"

Revival is not something we can work up, or produce ourselves. It must "come down" from God. So, if that is the case, then what is this thing we call "revival?"

Well, sometimes, in our quest to discover what something is, it is helpful if we can first establish what it is not:

A. Revival is not just a week of meetings.

This seems to be the most common idea about what revival is. You get a preacher and guest singer. You do some advertising. You make up some posters and put them around town. You throw in some gimmicks like bubble gum for the kids, a local rock band and pizza for the youth, swallow a goldfish or two for high attendance, and you have a week of meetings. When it's over, people ask, "How did the revival go?" And you get answers like:

--The preacher was great; funny; loud; hard; long-winded, etc.

--The music was awesome; too loud; too worldly; too showy, etc.

--The church was packed every night!

--We didn't have anybody saved, but two people came to the altar on the last night.

Notice that all of these answers are about the personalities on the platform, or the number of people who attended, but nothing is said about the power of God falling, people repenting of their sins or lives being changed. It is all superficial, man-caused, and man-centered. In a couple of days, everything will go back to business as usual.

B. Revival is not just excitement and an emotional experience.

People who know me say that I am an emotional person. Generally speaking, I think they are right. I get excited about the things that excite me and I am enthusiastic about the things and the people I love. So understand that I do not think there is anything wrong with showing emotion in your Christian life. I agree with D. Martin Lloyd-Jones when he says, *"There is nothing more useless than a merely formal Christian."* And the person who said, *"One person with passion is worth more than 10,000 persons with interest alone"* was spot-on when it comes to what it takes to influence others for Christ. It is a sad, but true assessment that too many Christians have lost the song in their heart, the smile on their face, the pep in their step, and the twinkle in their eye. They drag their Christianity around like a ball and chain, they spend very little time in prayer and Bible study, they rarely share their faith, there is little or no joy or enthusiasm in their Christian life, and for all practical purposes there is no difference between their lives and the lives of their unsaved neighbors.

That kind of Christianity is what led Mahatma Ghandi to say, " *If it weren't for Christians, I'd consider becoming a Christian."* Somebody once said that there were three kinds of Christians: shouters, doubters, and pouters. Which one are you? I'll take the shouter any day of the week! I do believe we ought to be excited about what Jesus Christ has done for us.

With that being said, let's just admit that just showing excitement and emotion does not mean you are experiencing genuine revival.

While true revival may be and often is accompanied by both excitement and emotion, the fact that the church may be jam-packed, that people are ecstatically clapping their hands, or even going to the altar at the invitation is not necessarily evidence that genuine revival has occurred. It may be the product of man-made manipulation techniques (I have seen this often), or merely remorse for the consequences of sin, rather than genuine repentance for the sin itself. It could also be an attention-seeking narcissist using the revival platform to get his attention fix. Sadly, I can say that I have seen all of these things in my 45 years of ministry.

But when genuine revival occurs, it is a beautiful thing to behold. When the Holy Spirit falls, the flesh has to go. The Spirit and the flesh are at odds with one another. Romans 8:5-8 says:

> *"For those who live according to the flesh set their minds on the things of the flesh, but those who live according to the Spirit, the things of the Spirit. For to be carnally minded is death, but to be spiritually minded is life and peace. Because the carnal mind is enmity against God; for it is not subject to the law of God, nor indeed can be. So then, those who are in the flesh cannot please God."*

Revival brings us once again to the foot of the Cross, and at the foot of the Cross, there is no room for boasting, bragging, or showboating. John Bisagno used to say, *"The Cross is an "I" crossed out!* What the "Laughing Revival" crowd never learned is that when true revival comes, the pulpit becomes a place of *execution* rather than a place of *exhibition*. In fact, I know a few Baptists who could stand to learn that lesson as well!

When the Holy Spirit is poured out upon a people in genuine Revival, He never leads them to frivolity and foolishness. No biblical revival ever started with "holy laughter," barking like dogs, howling like wolves, or stumbling around like a drunk person. These are counterfeits that tickle our ears and give us warm fuzzies and provide cheap entertainment. It is pure silliness and carnal worship that reeks of the flesh. It causes angels to weep and demons to rejoice as the holy things of God are made a mockery of. It is what led one woman to ask her pastor, "When are we going to stop entertaining the goats and get back to feeding the sheep?"

The so-called "Laughing Revival" that was borne out of the Toronto-Vineyard movement and culminated in the Pensacola Revival, made popular by the Kenneth Copelands, Benny Hinns, and Rodney Howard Brownes of the world make a complete mockery of genuine revival and holy things like repentance, confession of sin, purity, humility and intercession for souls. Instead the emphasis is on miracles, money, and showmanship. Things like gold dust falling from the ceiling, angel feathers, and slaying people in the Spirit border on the ridiculous and makes Christianity a laughing stock before the world. This is as far from biblical revival as Grape Nuts cereal is from either grapes or nuts.

Satan is the master counterfeiter, attempting to keep step with the work of God by distracting us and causing us to desire a "manifestation" of God rather that the very person of God. Jonathan Edwards said this:

"Satan will keep his grip on men as long as he can. But when he can do that no longer, he often tries to drive them to extremes. Satan wants them to dishonor God, and wound the Christian faith in that way."

Dr. Stephen Olford once said, *"Revival is not some emotion or worked-up excitement; it is an invasion from heaven that brings a conscious awareness of God."*

I am in lock-step with Michael Catt who said,

"We need to repent as long as we have religion without the Holy Spirit, Christianity without Christ, forgiveness without repentance, salvation without regeneration, and heaven without hell. And that's where we are! We've settled for Christianity Lite in America today. We have crowds, but where is the congregation? We have Starbucks in our Sunday School classes, but where is the Spirit? We are politically correct and socially active but spiritually dead! We live in a day of smooth talkers, stage lighting, and flattering tongues. And we don't know how to blush. Preachers are actually using vulgarity in the pulpit. They call it relevant; I call it repulsive. Props have replaced prayer. Preachers and churches are playing fast and loose with the Scriptures."

So revival is much more than just an emotional experience. It is a fresh pouring out of the Holy Spirit among the saints, and when that happens you cannot stay the same.

C. Revival is not evangelism

Now let me hasten to say that while it is 100% true that one of the greatest characteristics of genuine revival is the spontaneous and enthusiastic sharing of the gospel with sinners coming to Christ for salvation (this will be dealt with in a later chapter), revival and evangelism are not synonymous.

Revival is not the conversion of the local atheist, the town drunk, the local wife-beater, the drug dealer, some celebrity, or star athlete. That is Evangelism! Granted, these things can and do happen when true Revival comes, but there is a real difference between Revival and Evangelism. Someone has said that Evangelism is "down the aisle" while Revival is "across the aisle". In other words, in Evangelism sinners come down the aisle to be saved, while in Revival believers move across the aisles to get right with one another.

This, I believe, is the most common misconception of revival. Just think about it. What is the first question anyone asks when you tell them you've just had a revival meeting in your church? Is it not, "How many got saved?" We are conditioned to ask that question as if that is the only measurement of whether or not you've had genuine revival.

Vance Havner used to say, *"Many a so-called revival is only a drive for more church members, which adds more unsaved sinners, starched and ironed, but not washed, to a fellowship where even the true believers have not been aroused for years."*

So, if genuine Revival is not just a week of meetings, or an intense emotional experience, or evangelism, then what is it exactly?

The word "Revival" comes from two Latin words: Re, meaning "again," and Vivo, meaning "to live," Revival means "to live again", or to "bring back to life." A lost person cannot be revived. He needs to be "vived" before he can ever be "revived." He needs to be saved, born again, regenerated in order to receive spiritual life for the first time! But revival means "to live *again.*"

Evangelism is the salvation of sinners.

Revival is the stirring of God's people to new life; to new dedication; to new commitment; to new surrender and a new love and passion for the Lord Jesus Christ.

Evangelism is bringing the lost to new life in Jesus Christ.

Revival is bringing the church of Jesus Christ to new life in Him.

The great 19th century Revivalist Charles G. Finney said, *"Revival is nothing but a new beginning of obedience to God."*

D.L. Moody's successor, R.A. Torrey said, *"Revival is furnishing someone for the Holy Spirit to work through."*

D.M. Panton said, *"Revival is the in-rush of the Spirit into a body that threatens to be a corpse."*

Anne Graham Lotz said, *"Personal revival is Jesus in you, around you, through you, under you, over you, before you, and behind you."*

Promise Keepers adopted this definition of revival: *"Revival is the extraordinary work of God among His people causing extraordinary results in and through the church."*

Those are great definitions of revival. You see, when we are first saved, we are so on fire for Jesus we feel like we could charge Hell with a squirt pistol! We are like the young man who was asked one day if he knew for sure he was saved, and he answered, *"I sure do! I'm so saved I could swing over Hell on a rotten corn stalk singing 'Amazing Grace, How Sweet the Sound!'"* Now that's pretty saved, wouldn't you agree?

But somewhere along the way in his spiritual life, this believer who has been made alive in Jesus Christ and is ready to swing over Hell on that rotten cornstalk will cross paths with the world, the flesh, and the devil, not to mention the "wet blanket committee" from his church. He will suddenly discover that everybody doesn't just fall in love with him because he has become a Christian. Someone will criticize him. Someone will ridicule him. He will wake up one day and realize that he is in the middle of a spiritual warfare. There will be battles to fight and he will win some and lose some. Along the way, he may allow a little sin in his life; he gets discouraged, disappointed, or disillusioned with his experience in Christianity. The next thing you know, he begins missing church, stops reading his Bible, and no longer enjoys spending time in prayer. He has lost his vitality; his passion for Christ. What was once a joy is now a drudgery. He is in a backslidden state. He hasn't lost his salvation, for that is an impossibility, but he has done just what the word "backslidden" implies—he has slidden backwards. He is no longer growing in the Lord. Richard Owen Roberts, in his classic book, *Revival,* defined backsliding this way:

"A backslider is a person who was once emptied of their own ways, and filled with the ways of God, but gradually allowed their own ways to seep back until they are all but empty of God and full of themselves again."

The Christian life is like a mountain climber climbing an ice mountain. There is no standing still. As soon as you stop moving forward, you start sliding backward. You are either going forward, or you are going backward. The Christian life is like that. It is a relationship. Either you are getting closer to Christ or you are getting farther away from Him. There is no middle ground. And if you are wondering by now if you, yourself could possibly be backslidden, here is a question for you to ask: *Has there ever been a time in my life when I was closer to Jesus and more passionate about Him than I am at this very moment?* If so, guess what? You are backslidden. That's the very definition of the word. You have slidden backwards in your Christian life. You need revival.

And is it possible that's where the majority of church members are today? They are either lost, or in dire need of revival. But here's the good news: God is a loving, and merciful God who wants to revive your heart right now more than you want it revived. As Simon Peter discovered, He is willing to take you back even after you've denied him. We have often scowled at Judas Iscariot for betraying his Lord for 30 pieces of silver, but I know a lot of Christians who have betrayed Him for much less than that! The good news is that Jesus approached Simon Peter on the shore of Galilee according to John

21 and said, "Peter, I want you back." Have you ever wondered why Jesus asked Peter three times, "Peter, do you love me?" How many times did Peter deny Jesus? Think about it. He denied Jesus three times, and felt like he was unworthy to be a disciple any longer. So Jesus gave Peter three opportunities to reaffirm his love for his master. In essence, Jesus was saying, "Peter, I know you failed me, but I still love you. I want you back." And Peter returned in his love for Jesus, and was more mightily used of God after he had failed than before. That's what revival can do for you!

No matter how far you have drifted, how cold your heart has become, or how much you may have denied Him, I want you to know that Jesus wants you back. He can revive your heart and restore your joy, if you'll only let Him. Like the Prodigal Son who woke up one day in the hog pen of life, realized what a mistake he had made in leaving the Father's house, and even though he knew he didn't deserve to be forgiven went running back home only to see his father running toward him with open arms, would you be willing to turn back to the Father and be reconciled to Him"?

Learn the glorious lesson both Simon Peter and the Prodigal Son learned:

No matter what you've done, or how you've failed, **Jesus wants you back!**

3

DO WE REALLY NEED REVIVAL?

"Perhaps the church is not suffering for the sins of the world as much as the world is suffering for the sins of the church."--Dr. Erwin Lutzer

Del Fehsenfeld, Jr. founded Life Action Ministries, one of the greatest Revival ministries in America back in the 1971 in Buchanon, Michigan. Del, an anointed preacher of the gospel, liked to ask this question:

"If revival depended on me—my prayers, my faith, and my obedience—would America ever experience revival?"

What a powerful and convicting question! But no doubt, there are some who might hear that question and wonder, "Do we really need revival?" Aren't we doing okay, in light of the circumstances?"

I think the answer to that question is obvious to any thinking, discerning person who is watching the state of things in our nation right now. Many of our churches are dying a slow, agonizing death. And this was taking place long before the Pandemic hit. This has been taking place for decades. Many of our churches are like the proverbial frog in the boiling pot. They are dying a slow, agonizing death, moment by moment, degree by degree. They just don't realize it. We need to wake up to our need for revival.

How do we know that we need revival in America?

- Over 4,000 churches die and close their doors every year.
- 1500 pastors leaven the ministry for good every month!
- 50 pastors walk away from their churches every single day.
- Studies show that only 1 out of 10 pastors who attend seminary will retire in any type of vocational ministry.
- 8 out of 10 of our churched youth walk away from their faith in the first year of college.
- Since 1950, there are 30% fewer churches for today's population.
- North America is the only continent in the world where Christianity is not growing.
- 3,500 people leave the church every day in the U.S.
- According to studies by the Association of Church Missions Committee, 250,000 of the 300,000 U.S. Protestant congregations are either stagnant or dying.
- Giving per person in the church is proportionately less today than it was during the Great Depression.
- The U.S. is the number two missionary-*receiving* country in the world, behind Brazil. This is how our brothers and sisters around the world view our commitment to Jesus Christ and the spiritual health of the American church.
- For many years the Southern Baptist Convention has been considered the leader of the world in Evangelism and Missions. So how is the SBC doing in light of the cultural shift away from Christianity?
- The SBC is coming off a decline in membership for 14 years in a row.
- For those 14 years the SBC has averaged losing 200,000 members a year.
- In 2019 the SBC lost 288,000 members.
- In 2020, the SBC lost 435,632 members.
- Since 2019 the SBC has had a 47.76% decline in baptisms,

placing us at a low not experienced since the 1918 influenza pandemic.
- In a recent year, 9,000 SBC churches baptized no one. Another 14,000 churches baptized no one under age 18. That means that of our 51,500 churches, 25,000 of them baptized no one under the age of 18.
- In the SBC in 2019, the average number of baptisms in churches was 2.

These facts, as shocking as they are, are just indicators of how far we have drifted from God in our nation. Some are saying that it is possible we have crossed the line of no return. That it's too late for America. Others say that God has his hand on this nation like no other, has made us the leader of the free world, and nothing can destroy us. What do I believe? I believe we are moving at breakneck speed on a collision course with the return of the Lord Jesus Christ and His judgment and if we don't repent and return to God, America may not even be here when Christ returns! Study the eschatological passages of Scripture and see if you can find America in the end times. I can't! It has been said that *"Christianity will survive without America, but America cannot survive without Christianity."* We need revival! And not for convenience or for church growth, but for survival! It is revival for survival!

Claude King points out an interesting verse in the book of Malachi. It is Malachi 1:10 and it says,

> *"Oh, that one of you would shut the temple doors, so that you would not light useless fires on my altar! I am not pleased with you,"* says that Lord Almighty, *" and I will accept no offering from your hands."*

Why was God angry with Israel at this time? They were offering polluted sacrifices on the altar, giving God half-hearted worship, and living with a mediocre commitment. Sound familiar? Like so many in America today, they were just going through the motions. And God said, "I wish someone would lock the doors of the church so that you couldn't even come in to worship! I would rather you not worship at all, if all you have to offer is mediocrity.

Someone needs to tell the church today that mediocrity is *not* a fruit of the Spirit. A Christian who is half-hearted, half- baked, and half-stepping is a liability to Christianity and Evangelism. Yet that is the state of so many Christians in the church today. Many of our churches are just going through the motions Sunday after Sunday. They are the frozen chosen. There is no fire. No power. No joy. No oomph! Their favorite color is beige, their favorite gear is neutral and they're dying from sameness. Their Christianity is as dry as dust, as cold as ice, and as dead as King Tut. One pastor who complained about the coldness of his services said, "My church is so cold that if a Jersey milk cow came down the aisle she'd be giving out popsicles before she ever got to the front!"

Someone said, "If the joy of the Lord is our strength, then most churches couldn't whip a sick rabbit!" Like the worshippers in Malachi 1:13 that God took to task, they say, *"Oh, what a weariness!"*

Yes, we need revival! I believe it is the greatest need in the church today. And for revival to take place in America, it must first take place in the church! Revival never starts on the outside of the church and then breaks in. It always starts on the inside and breaks out. Revival can never happen in the world before it happens in the church of the Lord Jesus Christ. It can never change the world before it changes the church.

In the Old Testament, God wanted to save the city of Nineveh and called Jonah to go and preach repentance and salvation to them. But Jonah had no love for the Ninevites and refused to go. Instead, he went the exact opposite direction. He went down to Joppa and boarded a ship going to Tarshish. That's the exact opposite direction of Nineveh. God had to send a great storm and have Jonah thrown overboard by the sailors and swallowed by a great fish before Jonah came to his senses. In the belly of the fish (Is this a whale of a tale, or a tale of a whale?), Jonah repented and told God he was willing to go to Nineveh and preach repentance and salvation to them. When he did, revival broke out and the entire city was converted!

Now, here's the point I want to make. The greatest hindrance to revival coming to Nineveh, was not Nineveh. It wasn't the sinfulness of the Ninevites, or the the corruption of the politicians, or the immorality of the people, or the brutality of the police that was the obstacle for Nineveh to be converted. It was not even the practice of false worship and the presence of cults that stood in the way of revival. All of those things were present in Nineveh, just as they are in America, but those things were not the biggest obstacle to the great revival in Nineveh. The biggest obstacle to the salvation of Nineveh was Jonah! The prophet of God. When Jonah finally repented of his disobedience and indifference, Revival came. Jonah was the key to revival in Nineveh and God's people are the key to revival in our nation and in the world. That's why we must have revival. And that's why it must start in the church.

I memorized a poem a couple of years ago about Jonah and Nineveh: It goes like this:

> "Jonah built a little booth, a shelter from the heat;
> And a gourd vine grew, protection from the wind
>   that on him beat.
> Now Jonah rejoiced exceeding glad for that
>   convenient gourd,
> Especially since that comfort was provided by the
>   Lord.
>
> I thank you, Lord, you've been so good to my dear
>   wife and me
> We're glad we're in this peaceful land of great
>   prosperity.
> It makes us feel so very good, this little bungalow;
> The living room, the kitchenette, the rug, so soft, you
>   know.

> And we love our children every one, we keep them
>   home for God,
> The homeland needs them just as much as mission
>   fields abroad.
>
> And good Southern Baptists are we, my children,
>   wife and I
> So grateful that we're saved by grace, and secure
>   until we die,
> Uh, what's that Lord? Nineveh? Well, that's a
>   different thing.
> Right now we want to praise you, Lord, and to your
>   glory sing!
>
> And so, good ole Southern Baptist Jonahs, to the
>   Lord their praises tell.
> They sing, "We're saved and satisfied "… while
>   Nineveh goes to Hell!"

The truth that stands out here is that it is often our own church members and leaders that is holding back revival. Some revival leaders say that if just the spiritual leaders in the church would repent and get thoroughly right with God, we would have a revival like the world has never seen!

Dr. J. Edwin Orr, one of the world's greatest revival scholars, said that all revivals in history have come when anywhere from 1 to 11 Christians got completely right with God. That is an encouraging word!

I would like to close this chapter with a list of 25 evidences of a backslidden people as given by another well-known authority on revival, Richard Owen Roberts, and I warn you—this list is deeply convicting. Read it at your own risk.

Revival is needed....

- When prayer ceases to be a vital part of a professing Christian's life.
- When the quest for biblical truth ceases and one grows content with knowledge of eternal things already acquired.
- When biblical knowledge possessed or acquired is treated as external fact and not applied inwardly.
- When earnest thought about eternal things ceases to be regular and gripping.
- When services of the church lose their delights.
- When pointed discussions are an embarrassment.
- When sports, recreation and entertainment are a large and necessary part of your lifestyle.
- When sins of the body and of the mind can be indulged without an uproar in your conscience.
- When aspirations for Christ-like holiness cease to be dominant in your life and thinking.
- When the acquisition of money and goods becomes a dominant part of your life thinking.
- When you can mouth religious songs and words without heart.
- When you can hear the Lord's name used in vain, spiritual concerns mocked, and eternal issues flippantly treated and not be moved to indignation or action.
- When you can watch degrading movies and television and read morally debilitating literature.
- When breaches of peace in the brotherhood are of no concern to you.
- When the slightest excuse seems sufficient to keep from spiritual duty and opportunity.
- When you become content with your lack of spiritual power and no longer seek repeated endowments of power from on high.
- When you pardon your own sin and sloth by saying the Lord understands and remembers that we are but dust.
- When there is no music in your soul and no song in your heart.

- When you adjust happily to the world's lifestyle.
- When injustice and human misery exist around you, and you do little or nothing to relieve the suffering.
- When your church has fallen into spiritual declension and the Word of God is no longer preached there with power, and you are still content.
- When the spiritual condition of the world declines around you and you cannot perceive it.
- When you find yourself rich in grace and mercy and marvel at your own godlikeness.
- When you are willing to cheat your employer.
- When your tears are dried up and the hard, cold spiritual facts of your existence cannot unleash them.

When I read this list, I am reminded of something Vance Havner said long ago, *"Sunday morning Christianity is the greatest hindrance to true revival. There has never been a real work of God that did not result in heartburn alongside the hallelujahs."*

I must confess that every time I read this list it gives me heartburn alongside my hallelujahs. It convicts me and drives me to my knees to cry out to God for mercy.

Do we really need revival in America today? There can be no question that we do.

- We need revival to bring the church of the Lord Jesus Christ back to New Testament Christianity and release the power of God in our nation.
- We need revival to sanctify and cleanse us by bringing us once again to the foot of the cross.
- We need revival to heal our land.
- We need revival to empower us with the power of the Holy Spirit rather than clever human remedies and gimmicks.
- We need revival to save our families, our teens and our children.
- We need revival to sweep away all that does not glorify God

in our lives and in our churches, which are really *His* churches, leaving us transfixed on Him alone.
- We need revival so that God is acknowledged, worshipped, and obeyed and so that He can display His glory.
- We need revival so that we who call ourselves Christians can fall in love with Jesus all over again.

The church at Ephesus in Revelation 2 had a lot going for it. They were doing a lot of things right, but Jesus said to them,

> *"Nevertheless I have this against you, that you have left your first love. Remember therefore from where you have fallen, repent and do the first works, or else I will come to you quickly and remove your lampstand from its place---unless you repent."* (Revelation 2:4-5)

It's easy to lose the simplicity of Christianity. An AT&T commercial says, in reference to their phone service, "It's not complicated." Christianity, when broken down in its simplest form is not complicated. It's very simple. It's just loving Jesus, trusting Jesus, following Jesus, and serving Jesus. It may sound cliché-ish, but it's so true…

It's not about you.

It's not about me.

It's not about us.

It's not about the building.

It's not about the music.

It's not about the programs.

It's not about the budget.

It's not about any of those things.

It's all about Him.

His name is Jesus.

And He is Lord!

The Great Maestro, Arturo Toscanini, conducted Beethoven's 9th Symphony with a massive orchestra some years ago. The performance was breathtaking and flawless. When it was over, the crowd rose to their feet in a thunderous ovation. For ten minutes the crowd cheered as the standing ovation continued. Toscanini, filled with emotion, turned to his orchestra and whispered to them, "You. Are. Nothing!" Well, that was nothing new as Toscanini was known for berating his musicians. But then he said something no one expected. He said, "Toscanini. Is. Nothing. Ah! But Beethoven! Beethoven is everything! Everything! Everything!"

True revival brings me back to the realization that in myself, I am nothing.

In yourself, you are nothing.

In ourselves, we are nothing.

But Jesus! He is everything! Everything! Everything!

And that's why we need revival.

Revival brings us back to that one blessed truth. Jesus is everything!

The story is told of a very wealthy Englishman who had one of the greatest collections of priceless art in the world. He had only one son, and he was killed in the British Air Force in the war. When the old man died, they held an estate sale to auction off his priceless art collection. People came from all over the world to get a chance to purchase some of his beautiful art pieces. The air was electrified with excitement as the auctioneer stepped to the podium. He addressed the audience saying, "The will states that before any other piece of art can be sold, the first piece to be auctioned will be a hand painted portrait of his son as a little boy."

When the portrait of the little boy was unveiled, no one recognized the name of the artist, and the painting was not a very good one. No one even wanted to bid on it. The participants seemed to be put out that they were having to waste their time on this mediocre portrait of the boy. But sitting in the very back of the room was an old man who had once been the gardener for the owner. He had fond memories of the little boy and thought it would be nice to have the picture of him. He had very little money, but since no one else bid on the picture, he made a bid, and won it. As soon as he won it, the auctioneer brought his gavel down on the podium and announced, to everyone's shock that the auction was now over. They gasped in surprise and demanded to know why. The auctioneer said, "The owner's will further states that whoever gets the picture of the son, gets the whole lot."

Do you see the meaning? God has told us, "Whoever gets the Son, gets the whole lot." If you have Jesus, you have it all. Ron Dunn used to tell us,

"Jesus is all you need. Bu you may never know Jesus is all you need until Jesus is all you have. And when Jesus is all you have, you realize that He's all you ever needed anyway."

That is why we need revival. Revival is just falling in love with Jesus all over again.

II

TEN CHARACTERISTICS OF GENUINE REVIVAL

Send a Great Revival

Coming now to Thee O Christ my Lord,
Trusting only in Thy precious Word
Let my humble prayer to Thee be heard
And send a great revival in my soul.

Chorus: Send a great revival in my soul (in my soul)
Send a great revival in my soul (in my soul)
Let the Holy Spirit come and take control
And send a great revival in my soul.

Send the Holy Spirit now within
Burning out the dross and guilt of sin
Let Thy mighty works of grace begin
Oh, send a great revival in my soul

(Chorus)

Send a great revival, Lord, in me

Help me that I may rejoice in Thee
Give me strength to win the victory
And send a great revival in my soul

(Chorus)

Help me go for Thee, dear Lord, today
To some lonely soul that's gone astray
Help me lead them in the homeward way
Oh, send a great revival in my soul

(Chorus)

4

CHARACTERISTIC # 1 REPENTANCE

A DEEP CONVICTION OF PERSONAL SIN THAT LEADS TO REPENTANCE.

"You cannot repent too soon, because you do not know how soon may be too late."
--Thomas Fuller

When the Holy Spirit is poured out in revival, the first thing He does is to bring conviction of sin. Jesus told us in John 16:8 that when the Holy Spirit comes, He will convict the world of sin, of righteousness, and of judgment. Now that is a three-point sermon in one verse! But it begins with a conviction of sin. There has never been a revival apart from a deep conviction and repentance of sin.

We must remember that the name of the third person of the Trinity is "Holy" Spirit. So the "Holy" Spirit is obviously going to be concerned with our holiness. There is nothing in the Bible that associates laughter, silliness, and falling down like drunk people with genuine revival. There is much in the Bible that associates conviction, confession, and heartfelt repentance with genuine revival. So the very first thing that happens when the Holy Spirit is poured out upon a people or a church that is seeking God for revival is that He leads them to a heartfelt repentance, which produces a change in character, and a change in character ultimately leads to a change in lifestyle.

The fact of the matter is, one simply cannot be the same once revival comes. In the Welch Revival, the bars closed down, police stations and courts shut down for lack of crime, policemen and judges formed singing quartets to occupy their time, the churches were on fire for Christ, people were being saved by the thousands, and even the mules had to be retrained because they could not recognize the voice of their owners since they were no longer using profanity! Genuine revival produces change because of deep conviction and repentance of sin.

At this point, it might be good to define some terms that I will be using quite often in the next few chapters:

Repentance. The Greek word is *"Metanoia."* It is used over 100 times in the New Testament and it means "a change of mind that leads to a change of direction." The Prodigal Son of Luke 15 gives us a clear picture of repentance. In Acts 3:19-20, Simon Peter says, *"Repent, therefore, and turn back, that your sins may be blotted out, that times of refreshing may come from the presence of the Lord..."*

Confession. The Greek word is *"Homelogeo"* and it means "to say the same thing as." When we confess our sins we say the same thing about the sin that God says about it. This sin is putrid. It is ugly. It is damaging, and it does not belong in my life at all. I don't have to obey it. I am not in bondage to it. It should be put out of my life right now. I John 1:9 says, *"If we confess our sins, He is faithful and just to forgive our sins, and to cleanse us from all unrighteousness."*

Conviction. The Greek word is *"Elenxei."* It means "to convince; to prove; to rebuke." It is used in John 16:8 of the Holy Spirit. *"And when He is come, He will convict the world of sin, and of righteousness, and of judgment."*

Why are these terms important? Because when the Spirit is poured out and genuine revival comes, all three of these things will take place. There will inevitably be conviction of sin by the Holy Spirit, which will then lead to confession and repentance. Souls will be saved, Christians will be revived, and churches that have been cold and dead will come alive with the Spirit of God!

It was John Wesley who said, *"Give me 30 men who love nothing but God, hate nothing but sin, and seek only the glory of God, and I will set the world on fire!"*

So why is it we hear precious little about repentance today? Is it because it makes us uncomfortable? Is it because we just don't want to change? Is it because our church members won't like us as much if we preach that way? Religious people have never liked the message of repentance, by the way. Just ask John the Baptist. It cost him his head. (Matthew 14:1-12)

I love the way James McDonald talks about the message of repentance, when he says:

"I would love it if I could preach a one-word message the way the Old Testament prophets sometimes did."

"Good morning. **REPENT!** *Let's pray."*

How great would that be? And they ALL preached the same message—every one of them. It was plagiarism to the max!

"Good morning. **REPENT!***"*

Then they'd get in their chariot and ride across town:

"Hello. **REPENT!***"*

"How are you, today, ma'am? **REPENT!***"*

"Nice turban, sir. **REPENT!***"*

Now why did all these Old Testament prophets preach this same message? It was because they knew that the good things God is longing to give us, willing to give us, and ready to give us are released into our lives when we repent.

And lest you think that's just the Old Testament, and things were different in the New Testament, let me remind you that the Gospels record that John the Baptist's message was a simple one: *"Repent, for the Kingdom of Heaven is at hand!"* (Matt. 3:2) Our Lord Jesus came out of the wilderness with the Spirit of God on Him and in Him and the Bible says, *"From that time Jesus began to preach and to say, 'Repent, for the Kingdom of Heaven is at hand."*

And then there's the early church in Acts 2 on the Day of Pentecost, and the very first message preached by the Apostle Peter as the Holy Spirit was poured out. Can you guess what His message was about? Surely he preached about God's "Amazing Grace," right? Surely, he took advantage of the moment to tell them how to have "their best life now," right? No! He preached Repentance. Then, in Acts 3 he preached it again. Surely he wouldn't preach the same message two Sundays in a row, would he? Wrong again! In Acts 3:19, Peter says, *"Repent, therefore, and turn back that your sins may be blotted out, that times of refreshing may come from the presence of the Lord."*

So, here's an interesting question: If repentance was such a vital message in both the Old and the New Testament, then why isn't anyone preaching that message today? How come we never hear about repentance from the pulpit? Oh! I get it! It must be because we have *less* sin in our lives today than First Century Jewish people did in theirs.

Riiiiight!

We have evolved into better people so that message would not be relevant today, I guess. Do you honestly think there is *less* sin in the nation or in the church today than there was in the first century Jewish church? Or could it be that we have so watered down the message of repentance out of a desire to be politically correct or maybe out of a sense of "self-preservation," that we just don't mention it because it would not be personally expedient to do so?

The great preacher, Joseph Parker, once said, *"The man whose little sermon is "repent" sets himself against his age and will, for the time being, be battererd mercilessly by the age whose moral tone he challenges. There is but one end for such a man—"off with his head!" You had better not try to preach repentance until you have pledged your head to heaven!"*

If that is true, then it is easy to understand why preachers are hesitant to preach on sin and call for repentance. But still, after all is said and done, we must take courage, remember that our calling is not to create the message, just to deliver it. So we must "pledge our heads to heaven," preach the message, and let the chips fall where they may. At the end of the day, wouldn't you rather lay your head on your pillow knowing that you have pleased your Heavenly Father, even if it meant disappointing and angering a few people, rather than pleasing a few people, and disappointing your Heavenly Father?

But since there can be no revival without confession and repentance, we must get over our fears of being rejected, and preach repentance. It is Biblical!

The message of the Old Testament prophets was ... REPENT!

When John the Baptist went out preaching, his message was ... REPENT!

When our Lord started His ministry, His message was ... REPENT!

When He sent the disciples out, they preached ...REPENT!

On the Day of Pentecost, Peter preached ... REPENT!

When Paul was in Athens, his message was ... REPENT!

The last thing our Lord said to the church was not the Great Commission, but ... REPENT!

The last thing the average church member is willing to do today is ...REPENT!

Granted, repentance is not a politically correct term. It doesn't make you feel all warm and fuzzy. To insinuate that we are not as pristine and pure as we think we are is offensive to many. We just don't like the idea of repentance. Dealing with sin makes us uncomfortable. It has been said that most of us have denied Christ like Peter did, but few of us have wept bitterly in repentance like Peter did!

In his wonderful book, *The Power of Surrender*, Michael Catt says, *"If you are listening to a preacher or reading a Christian author who never uses the word 'repentance,' you need to change churches or start reading someone else. They aren't helping you. They have adjusted the gospel to be more acceptable. They have cut out the bold, prophetic voices of the Scripture."*

To be sure, preachers of repentance have not fared well in history. People do not like to be confronted with their sins. Just ask Martin Luther, John Wesley, Detreich Bonhoeffer, and Martin Niemoller.

Speaking of Martin Niemoller, you may not be aware of the fact that when Hitler came to power, he brought all the Protestant and Catholic Ministers in for a meeting. He told them, "You confine yourselves to the church. I will take care of the German people." No one challenged the Furher on this point. Silence filled the room until Pastor Niemoller stepped forward and said, *"I'm sorry, sir, but the Bible says we, as Pastors, are to take care of the people. They are our responsibility."* Hitler was furious. Over 1,000 churches took down their crosses on their buildings and replaced them with Hitler's Swastika. But not Niemoller. Hitler had it in for him and it wasn't long before he found an excuse to arrest him and put him in jail. Sometime later Hitler was touring his jails with some priests, and they came across the cell in which Pastor Niemoller and several others were being held. The priest recognized Niemoller and stepped up to the cell and said, *"Pastor Niemoller! What are **you** doing in there?"* To which Martin Niemoller responded, *"The question, Sir, is, 'What are you doing out there?'"*

Yes, if we stand for the truth, there may be a price to pay. If we preach the truth, there may be a price to pay. But if it was worth it for Isaiah, Jeremiah, Micah, Malachi, John the Baptist, Simon Peter, our Lord Jesus Christ, Paul the Apostle, Dietrich Bonheoffer, and Martin Niemoller, to stand for the truth, then we should stand for it too, no matter what the world may threaten to do to us!

We would do well to remember Pastor Niemoller's most famous quote:

> "First they came for the Socialists, and I did not speak out because I was not a socialist.
> Then they came for the trade unionists, and I did not speak out because I was not a trade unionist.
> Then they came for the Jews, and I did not speak out because I was not a Jew.
> Then they came for me, and there was no one left to speak for me."

It's important to take a stand for what is right, true, and biblical. You say, "But, isn't that being controversial?" Shouldn't we, as Christians, be peacemakers and avoid controversy at all costs? Let me say that there is nothing noble about controversy for the sake of controversy. But controversy for the sake of Truth is always noble. Do you know who the most controversial person to ever walk the face of the earth was? Jesus Christ! He was Truth in a human body! And everywhere He went, people were divided. They either loved Him, or they hated Him. They either wanted to worship Him, or they wanted to kill Him. He said, *"I am the Way, the Truth, and the Life."* (John 14:6) And when you met Jesus, you had to choose. You were either for Him, or against Him. There was no middle ground.

And, by the way, contrary to what many believe, Jesus *never* told us to be Peace *lovers*. He told us to be Peace *Makers*. There is a difference. Peace lovers want peace at any cost. Truth is irrelevant. We must *love* everybody, be nice, and get along. Peace makers, on the other hand, will be peaceable until truth is being compromised, at which point they will feel compelled by the Holy Spirit to stand up for the truth. For the Christian, it is never, "Peace at any cost." We are to be peacemakers unless there is a truth at stake, and then we must speak the truth in love (Ephesians 4:15) and stand firmly on the principles of God's Word. And let me add that standing firmly on God's Word is *not* a license for being arrogant, rude, or mean-spirited. We have all known Christians who knew the Bible forward and backwards, but their attitude was so rotten that no one could stand to be around them. We as Christians are famous for doing the right thing the wrong way. You may be right, but you will lose the argument, and maybe your testimony, if you become angry and condescending or have a stinky attitude.

When Jesus said, *"I came not to bring peace but a sword" (*Matt. 10:34) what did He mean? He meant that for those of us who follow him there are going to be times in our lives when we must stand up for the truth. To be counter-cultural. To swim against the stream. To cut across the grain. To do so means we must at times stand against some things. We must confront the world with the Truth. We must be salt and light. And, at times, it may be controversial. At times it may be unpopular. It may cost you something. But Jesus always warned his followers to "count the cost." We have to take up the Cross. We have to die to self. And when the time comes, we have to take a stand.

This is what led Jim Elliot, the martyred missionary to the Auca Indians, to pray *"Lord, don't let me be a sign post along the highway of life. Let me be a fork in the road so that when people see me they have to decide one way or another for Christ."*

Let's face it, we live in a pluralistic society where truth is sacrificed on the altar of relevance and tolerance. It is increasingly difficult to be a man or woman of conviction and be accepted by the world in which we live. Yet, we have this admonition in Romans 12:2 that says, *"Do not be conformed to this world, but be transformed by the renewing of your mind."* J.B. Phillips translates this verse this way, *"Don't let the world around you squeeze you into its mold."* Eugene Peterson's The Message says, *"Don't become so well-adjusted to your culture that you fit into it without even thinking."*

WHEN THE FIRE FALLS

At the Southern Baptist Convention in New Orleans, Louisiana in 1990, Dr. Adrian Rogers preached a powerful message on the prophet Micah in which he made some statements about truth that have challenged me to the core of my being. He said,

> *"It is better to speak a truth that hurts and then heals, than to speak a lie that comforts and then kills."*
>
> *"It is better to be hated for telling the truth than to be loved for telling a lie."*
>
> *"It is better to be divided by truth than to be united in error"*
>
> *"It is better to stand alone with the truth, than to be wrong with the multitudes."*
>
> *"It is better to ultimately succeed with the truth, than to temporarily succeed with a lie."*

As preachers of the Word, we must tell people the truth, no matter the consequence. We must be prophets, not politicians. Do you know the difference?

Politicians tell people what they want to hear, and take them where they want to go. Prophets tell people what they need to hear, and take them where they need to go. The nature of the ministry of a politician is that of compromise. The nature of the ministry of a prophet is that of conviction. A politician seeks to please people. A prophet seeks to please God.

But where, oh where, are God's prophets today?

People need to hear the message of repentance. So, as uncomfortable as it may make us to speak on the subject, we must do it because it is truth, and at the end of the day all that matters is Truth. So we must preach it! We must preach it with compassion, but we must preach it! We must preach it with tears, but we must preach it! The people may not like it, but we must preach it nonetheless! It was the message John the Baptist preached. It was the message Jesus preached. It was the message Peter preached. And it was the message Stephen preached. John the Baptist was beheaded. Jesus was crucified. Peter was crucified upside down. And Stephen was stoned. But they knew they had to preach the message.

The fact is, revival will *never* come without God's people becoming deeply aware of their own sin. The first step toward revival is a divine dissatisfaction with the status quo. If you are satisfied with your Christian life as it is, you will not see revival. Vance Havner used to say that the reason most Christians never experience revival is because they are content to live without it. There is only one thing that can keep you from experiencing revival, and that is sin. And there is only one kind of sin that can keep you from experiencing revival—*your* sin.

You see, we Christians have become very, very good at magnifying the sins of others while at the same time glossing over the sins of our own heart. We have a kind of "spiritual hyperopia;" a farsightedness, where things far off are very clear, but things close up are kind of blurry. So we can see the sins in others very clearly, but our own sins we are blind to. And correct me if I'm wrong, but didn't Jesus have something to say about that?

> *"Judge not, that ye be not judged. For with what judgment you judge, you will be judged; and with the measure you use, it will be measured back to you. And why do you look at the speck in your brother's eye, but do not consider the plank in your own eye? Or how can you say to your brother, 'Let me remove the speck from your eye'; and look, a plank is in your own eye? Hypocrite! First remove the plank from your own eye, and then you will see clearly to remove the speck from your brother's eye."*
>
> ---Matthew 7:1-5

Isn't it amazing how easy it is to judge others harshly, while at the same time being prone to justify, make excuses, downplay, blame others, play the victim, coddle and compromise with our own sins? But when the Holy Spirit is poured out in revival and He turns the spotlight of conviction on your heart, there is only one right thing to do: to confess and repent of our own sins.

Until the Holy Spirit convicts us, our sins seem small and we *think* we are doing all right. But that is because we are measuring ourselves by each other and that means we're using the wrong measuring stick! We look at others and think, "Well, I'm not so bad. Look at how they're living." But when we stand before God some day, we're not going to be measured against Joe Blow down the road, or some nominal church member, or carnal Christian. We're going to be measured by the pure, perfect and thrice holy Son of God!

The English Reformer, John Bradford, is credited with the saying, *"There but for the grace of God, go I,"* but few know the background story to that quote. John Bradford was a powerful preacher and theologian in the early 16th century. One Sunday he was preaching to a crowd under a large oak tree when a procession of soldiers came by escorting a prisoner to a tree to be hanged for his crimes. Bradford stopped preaching and the crowd fell silent as the somber procession passed by. John Bradford then made the now famous statement, *"There, but for the grace of God, go I."* He was saying what Paul said in I Corinthians 15:10, and what is true of each one of us, *"…I am what I am by the grace of God…"* He was later imprisoned in the Tower of London for supposed crimes against Mary Tudor. (They were bogus). Yet he was burned at the stake for his testimony for Christ in 1555.

Sometime ago I read about a family traveling north on vacation. They passed a field with some sheep in it. The little girl exclaimed, "Look, mommy, at how white that sheep looks!" On their way back, it had begun to snow and the ground was covered in beautiful snow. The little girl saw the same sheep and said, " Oh mommy, look how dirty that sheep has gotten!" Well, the first time she saw the sheep against the background of dirt and grass and it looked white. But the second time she saw the same sheep against the snowy white background and it looked dirty. Against the dirty background of the field, the sheep looked clean. But against the brilliant white background of the snow, the sheep looked dirty. That's the difference in measuring ourselves against another sinner and measuring ourselves against the snowy white character of the Son of God.

In genuine revival, when confronted with the holiness of God and attracted to the light of the life of God, we become acutely aware of the sin in our lives. (See Isaiah 6:1-5 and 2 Corinthians 7:10-11)

Have you ever gone into a room that is dark and opened the blinds to let the light in, and suddenly you could see thousands of tiny particles of dust just floating in the air? Where did they come from? Did the light cause them? No. They were there the whole time, you just couldn't see them until the light exposed them.

That's how it is with revival. Suddenly we can clearly see sins that we couldn't see before. They were there all along, we just didn't notice them. But when the Holy Spirit comes, He convicts of sin. Even so-called "little" sins. And that is why one of the first characteristics of revival is confession of sin and repentance.

I used to have a mistaken notion that the closer to God I got, the less sin I would have to confess. I used to dream of a time when I would be so close to God that I hardly ever had a need to confess sin. But then I became acquainted with some people who were much closer to God than I was. I was surprised at how sensitive to sin they were! They were confessing things that I thought were so small they didn't even register as sin! Godly people are quick to confess sins that others may overlook. Why? Because they are closer to the Light, and therefore sin is much more quickly exposed. It works like this:

The closer to God I get, the more spiritual light shines into my life.

The more spiritual light that shines into my life, the more sin is exposed. (remember those dust particles?)

The more sin is exposed, the more sin I need to confess.

The more sin I confess, the more cleansing takes place.

The more cleansing that takes place the more full of the Spirit I become.

The more full of the Spirit I become the more like Jesus I am.

And there you have it! The end game of repentance and revival is to be like Jesus!

God has promised to forgive anything we will confess as sin. (I John 1:9) That's called grace! And here is the good news: **There is more grace in Christ than there is sin in me! Hallelujah!** Just take a minute and let that statement sink in. It is so encouraging and liberating!

John Avant, in his diary of the revival that broke out at Coggins Avenue Baptist Church in Brownwood, TX in the mid 1990's, said they were seeing "an open cry of desperation." An open and unashamed crying in great repentance, even brokenness before the Lord. He said, *"Real, life-changing repentance is becoming the common thread of experience in increasing numbers of student groups, churches, and meetings of God's people, especially among the leaders."* This amazing pouring out of God's Spirit overflowed from his church and made a deep impact on Howard Payne University and Southwestern Baptist Theological Seminary.

Nancy Leigh DeMoss has said,

> *"Revival is not just another emphasis to add to our already overcrowded agendas. It's not an option. It's not just a nice idea. A meeting with God in genuine revival is our only hope, our church's only hope, our nation's only hope."*

Back in the 1990's when Promise Keepers was going strong, the staff of Promise Keepers was praying for Revival when one of the men suddenly broke into tears, sobbing, and continuing for some time. When he finally stopped, he started to sing an old hymn. Here is what he sang:

> Pass me not, O gentle Savior, hear my humble cry;
> While on others Thou art calling, do not pass me by.
> Savior, Savior, hear my humble cry;

> While on others Thou art calling, do not pass
> me by."

My friend, can I make a personal appeal to you right now? YOU are the revival that God is seeking! Don't allow Him to pass you by today. Would you put this book aside for a few minutes, get down on your knees and like Jacob of old, just cling to Him and say, "I won't let you go until you bless me!" Don't allow God to leave until you are changed.

Would you join with me and many others who are crying out to God and pleading for revival? Would you ask Him to begin something new and fresh in your heart and in your church? If you will, He will come to you and bless you, forgive you, cleanse you and fill you with His Holy Spirit! And today, Revival will be yours!

As Miss Bertha Smith used to say, "*You don't have to ask God to bless you. He's already decided to do that. You just have to get blessable!*"

Ladies and gentlemen, let's get blessable!

5

CHARACTERISTIC # 2 BROKENNESS

BROKENNESS AND HUMILITY BEFORE THE LORD

"Brethren! When we get humble enough, and low enough, and desperate enough, and hungry enough, and concerned enough, and passionate enough, and broken enough, and clean enough, and prayerful enough, **then** *God will send us a revival that equals and surpasses the awakening this country experienced in the days of Charles Finney!"*
--Leonard Ravenhill, in Sodom Had No Bible

In seasons of genuine revival when the Spirit is being poured out on a people, confession and repentance is followed by a spirit of humility and brokenness before the Lord. This brokenness and humility is highly valued by God.

Do we really understand that there is one thing that God hates every time He sees it? Not just some of the time. Not 99.5% of the time. Not just on Tuesdays and Wednesdays. He hates something all of the time. And I don't mean He's just displeased with it, or that it just upsets Him. I mean He *hates* it! He's opposed to it. He comes up against it.

He hated it when He saw it in the Old Testament.

He hated it when He saw it in the New Testament.

He hates it when He sees it in an individual.

He hates it when He sees it in a nation.

He hates it when He sees it in a preacher.

He hates it when He sees it in a husband

He hates it when He sees it in a wife.

He hates it when He sees it in a teen.

He hates it when He sees it in an angel.

He hates it when He sees it in you.

He hates it when He sees it in me.

He hates it 100% of the time.

I'm talking about God! The God of the Universe! The God of love!

There is something that God hates all of the time, and that something is **Pride!**

God hates Pride!

Now that's the bad news. But let me tell you the good news.

There is something that God responds to all of the time. He loves it! Not just 99.5% of the time. Not just on Tuesdays and Wednesdays. He loves it all of the time.

He loved it when He saw it in the Old Testament.

He loved it when He saw it in the New Testament.

He loves it when He sees it in an individual.

He loves it when He sees it in a nation.

He loves it when He sees it in a preacher.

He loves it when He sees it in a husband.

He loves it when He sees it in a wife.

He loves it when He sees it in a teen.

He loves it when He sees it in an angel.

He loves it when He sees it in you.

He loves it when He sees it in me.

He loves it 100% of the time.

There is something that God loves and responds to every time He sees it, and that something is **Humility!**

The Bible is clear from cover to cover that God hates and rejects pride, but He loves and responds to humility.

The Bible has plenty to say about the sin of pride. Proverbs 6:16-19 gives us the 7 things on God's hit list of sins that He hates. Guess which one tops the list? "A proud look." Have you ever wondered why pride seems to be singled out as the sin God hates the most? It is the sin of Satan, that's why. It was the very first sin. Long before Adam and Even sinned in the Garden, Lucifer, the archangel of heaven, sinned and led one third of the angels in a rebellion against God. It didn't work, and Lucifer was kicked out of heaven.

Here is the answer to one of the most often asked questions pastors get.

"Who created the devil?"

"If God created everything, does that mean He created the devil?"

"How could a good God create the devil?"

The answer to that question is: God did not create the devil. He created Lucifer, the most beautiful, wise, and talented being in the universe other than God Himself. He was the Archangel of Heaven, charged with the task of defending the very throne of God (Ezekiel 28:11-17). But the day came when Lucifer took his eyes off of God and put them on himself and his heart was lifted up in pride (Ezekiel 28: 2, 5, 15,17). This was the very first sin. And since rebellion is the child of pride, the very next thing he did was to attempt to overthrow the throne of God (Isaiah 14:12-15) God crushed the rebellion, cast Lucifer and the millions of angels that followed him out of heaven (Isaiah 14: 12; Ezekiel 28:16; Luke 10:18), and Lucifer became the devil. So, in actuality, God created Lucifer, and Lucifer made *himself* into the devil.

That is why God hates pride so much. That is why Jesus reserved his harshest words of judgment and criticism, not for the pagans of his day, not for the prostitutes and tax collectors, but for the Pharisees. They were full of pride. Jesus taught us to "...*beware of the leaven of the Pharisees.*" He was talking about pride. The best definition of pride I have ever come across is this: "Pride is taking credit for what, in reality, God and others have accomplished in my life." Humility, then, would be "joyfully giving the credit to God and others for anything good that is accomplished in my life." The apostle Paul said in I Corinthians 15:10 *"I am what I am by the grace of God."* Paul gave credit to God for all the good that had taken place in his life. So should we.

Corrie Ten Boom was once asked how she handled all the praise and accolades that people gave her because of her powerful work for God. She smiled and said, "When people come up and give me a compliment...I take each remark as if it were a flower. At the end of the day I lift up the bouquet of flowers I have gathered throughout the day and say, 'Here you are, Lord, it is all yours.'" God will not share His glory with anyone. He alone deserves to be worshipped and praised and glorified. And when we try to take credit for what He has done in our life, the Bible calls that pride.

God knows that we're a little bit like that woodpecker that was pecking on a pine tree. At that very moment, a bolt of lightning hit the pine tree and split it right down the middle. The woodpecker backed up, studied that pine tree for a bit, then flew away. In a few minutes, he flew back with seven other woodpeckers and said to them, "There it is boys! See, I told you!"

Sometimes, if we're not careful, we can be just like that woodpecker. We try to take credit for what only God could have done. We forget that we are nothing without Him.

We're like the ant riding on the back of the elephant as he crossed a swinging bridge. When they got to the other side, the ant said to the elephant, "We really made her swing that time, didn't we, big boy!"

Those are funny stories, but they make a good point. It is ridiculous for us to try to take credit for what only God can do in our life by His grace and power. The moment we begin to think we are something, and begin to brag a little, or steal a little of God's glory, the sweet dove of the Holy Spirit will take flight. God will not share His glory with anyone!

When true revival takes place, we find ourselves on our faces before God, repentant, humble, and broken. And as much as God hates to see pride in our lives, He just as much loves to see humility in our lives.

You are never more like Jesus than when you are giving the credit to others and the glory to God for the good things that are happening in your life. Giving the credit to others and the glory to God is the hallmark of humility. That is what Joseph was doing when he was receiving praise from Pharaoh for interpreting his dreams when no one else in the Kingdom could. He made this simple, but profoundly humble statement, "*It is not in me.*" (Genesis 41:16). What a great response! "*It is not in me.*" Simply stated, *that* is humility.

Do you know what the only self-description Jesus ever gave of himself was? It is found in Matthew 11:29, "*...I am meek and lowly at heart.*" Those two phrases sum up the character of Jesus Christ. Meek. Lowly at heart. They form a picture of humility. That's why I say that you are never more like Jesus than when you are giving the credit to others and the glory to God. When you are being humble.

And the converse is true as well: You are never more like the devil than when you are bragging and full of pride.

That's why I have told people for years, "Be careful of what you say to young preachers." "Son, you're going be the next Billy Graham." "You should be preaching on television." "Someday you're going to be preaching to thousands."

Don't do that. "Why not?" you say? Because, if you do, he might actually begin to believe that nonsense, and if he does, his heart is going to get full of pride thinking he's God's gift to preaching, and then God is going to have to break him, because God can only use broken vessels. I saw a book one day by a very popular Christian comedian, entitled, "God only uses cracked pots." It may have been a play on words, but it is absolutely true. A broken man is pliable, teachable, humble and usable and he's the only kind of man God is looking for.

Many years ago a missionary served in a region of Africa that had known seasons of true revival. Whenever he would mention the name of any Christian, the national believers would ask him, "Is he a *broken* Christian?"

They did not ask, "Is he a committed Christian?"

They did not ask, "Is he a knowledgeable Christian?"

They did not ask, "Is he a hard working Christian?"

They wanted to know, "Is he a *broken* Christian?"

Here is a question for you to consider. Are you a broken Christian? Am I? That is an important question to answer because there is nothing; absolutely nothing more beautiful to God; more usable to God; more pleasing to God than a Christian who has been broken.

What kind of heart does God revive? Isaiah gives us the answer, and that same thought is interwoven like a thread throughout the Word of God. Hear the prophet Isaiah in Isaiah 57:15:

> *"For thus says the High and Lofty One Who inhabits eternity, whose name is Holy;*
>
> *'I dwell in the high and holy place, with him who has a contrite and humble spirit, to revive the spirit of the humble, and to revive the heart of the contrite ones."*

According to this Scripture God has two "addresses." The first one we are familiar with. God lives in "eternity," in the high and holy place. But he also has another "address" and this is the one that amazes me. He dwells with those who have a humble and contrite spirit. The Hebrew word for "contrite" means to be "crushed like powder."

You know, most Kings are usually comfortable with the high and mighty, and the wealthy and successful. But this King, our King, the King of Kings chooses to dwell with those who are humble, broken and contrite. Wow!

We all love the Beatitudes of Matthew 5. They are the introduction to the greatest sermon ever preached in all of history—The Sermon on the Mount. But do you recall the very first point Jesus made in this magnificent sermon?

"Blessed are the poor in spirit, for theirs is the kingdom of heaven." The word "blessed" means "happy." So the first step to happiness and joy according to Jesus is to become humble. "Poor in spirit" does not mean you have poor posture, shuffle your feet and look down all the time. It's not having poor self esteem. It means you are utterly dependent upon God. You admit you don't have it all together, you haven't arrived, and you're not the sum total of the universe. To be "poor in spirit" means you realize you are spiritually bankrupt before God. Pride goes out the window! No more strutting. Did you know there are no peacocks in heaven? There is no room for strutting up there.

"In my hand, no price I bring, simply to the cross I cling." So says the famous hymn, *"Rock of Ages."* Revival cannot come as long as we sit in church in our glad rags, heady, haughty, and high-minded,

thinking we're doing God a wild favor by being there. So many church people are ego-maniacs strutting to Hell, thinking they're too good to be damned for all eternity. But when God begins a work of revival, He always begins with repentance, humility and brokenness.

My life verse is Psalm 34:18. It is one of the most beautiful and encouraging verses in the Bible. God revealed this verse to me the first time I experienced spiritual brokenness way back in 1984. I was pastoring my very first church at the ripe old age of 24. I had been called to pastor the church when I was 21. The church had grown exponentially in those first three years, but I wasn't mature enough to handle the success. I thought I was doing pretty good until God revealed me to me the way He saw me. Did you catch that? *God revealed me to me as He saw me.*

Mickey Bonner was a protégé of Manley Beasley, who was, in my opinion, one of the godliest men I have ever been privileged to know. In his groundbreaking book, *Brokenness, the Forgotten Factor of Prayer,* Mickey suggests a prayer that every Christian ought to pray every day. "Lord, reveal me to me as You see me." As soon as we pray that prayer, we are brought to the place of brokenness. We realize how far we have drifted from God's standard, and we relinquish the belief that we have arrived.

Mickey lived a life of brokenness. I was privileged to have him in my church for the last revival meeting he ever preached. He was 65 years old, and he was so spiritual he was scary. He preached with great power each night and on Thursday, I picked him up at his motel and could tell he was very excited about something. He had received a phone call the evening before from one of the greatest Christian teachers of the 1990's. He had been reading Mickey's book and invited him to speak at a conference in Knoxville, Tennessee two weeks after our revival. He was expecting between 15,000 and 20,000 people at this conference. Mickey was beside himself with excitement.

He was asked to speak on the subject of brokenness, which he did. At the end of his message, his closing statement was, "God wants all of us to be broken, because He can only use broken men and broken women." He then paused, blinked twice, and collapsed to the floor and died. He did not grimace, wince, or show any sign of pain or discomfort. Within just a few seconds several doctors and medical personnel who were in the audience were on the platform working on him, but it was too late. He had suffered a massive heart attack and may have been dead before he ever hit the floor. Mickey Bonner had preached his final message, and gone directly to heaven from the pulpit. They dismissed the people for the rest of the afternoon, but when they came back for the evening session, it was discovered that Mickey's suit jacket was still draped on the chair where he had been sitting on the platform. The conference leader simply held up the jacket and related the story of the mantle of Elijah falling on Elisha who had prayed for a double portion of the spirit that rested on Elijah to fall on him. He asked them to bow in prayer and ask God for a double portion of the spirit of brokenness that was on Mickey Bonner. At that very moment, the Spirit of God fell on that large audience and men and women alike fell on their knees all over that arena and began crying out to God in repentance over a lack of brokenness in their lives.

That's exactly what happened to me. I began to see how I was so full of pride, so full of self, and so full of sin. It was devastating to my ego. I was not the person, the husband, the father, or the pastor people thought I was. I was a hypocrite. Yes, my church was growing. Yes, we were baptizing right and left. Yes, the crowds were coming, and, yes, our church was the talk of the town. But what God showed me was that while I looked successful and "together" on the outside, I was a mess on the inside.

NEWSFLASH FOR PASTORS: **You may be popular and successful on the outside and your church may be growing like nobody's business, but if you are failing in your home, failing with your family, and failing in your personal life, you are failing in the eyes of God regardless of what your church is doing!** If you are not lovingly shepherding your first flock (your family), you cannot and will not effectively shepherd God's flock (His church)!

God showed me a clear picture of what I looked like on the inside, and it was not a pretty sight. My spiritual sloppiness and pride had done damage to my wife, my children, my home and my church. Although my church was growing, God was not pleased at all with the way I was treating my family. This revelation devastated me. I was broken, humbled, and distraught. I cancelled all my appointments and told our church secretary that I would not be in the office that day, and possibly for several days. I knew I could do nothing but stay in my closet and pray. I prayed that way for days. I spent most of those days in my closet (we had very large closets in our house at the time) seeking God and just crying out to God. I had never cried like that in all my life. God showed me my heart and how wretched it was.

I had never heard a sermon on brokenness. I had never read a book on brokenness. But I was experiencing it in full measure. And I didn't even know what to call it. Later that very year, Dr. Charles Stanley would come out with a series of cassette tapes called "The Blessings of Brokenness" and I would learn that what I was experiencing had a name. It was called Brokenness.

On one of those days while praying in my closet in the dark, I began to weep before the Lord. I believe it was the lowest I had ever felt. Suddenly, from out of nowhere, like a ray of light, these words popped into my head, "Read Psalm 34:18." I stopped praying and thought, "Where did that come from?" Then I heard it again. "Read Psalm 34:18." It was clear as a bell. Now, mind you, I didn't have a clue what Psalm 34:18 said! I didn't even know if there were 18 verses in Psalm 34. I jumped up, turned on the light in the closet, and flipped the pages of my Bible as fast as I could. I can vividly remember thinking how foolish I would feel if I got to Psalm 34 and there were only 10 or 12 verses there. And suddenly there it was. Psalm 34. And there were 22 verses in that Psalm! When I read verse 18, I was overwhelmed with what it said and the thought that God Himself had directed me to that verse. The presence of the

Holy Spirit in that closet was palpable. This was a God thing! God had actually spoken to me and led me to this beautiful verse promising that He is near me and will "save" those who were of a broken and contrite heart. For the first time in a week, I felt hope. Tears of despair turned to tears of joy as I read the verse over and over again:

"The Lord is nigh unto those who have a broken heart, and saves such as be of a contrite spirit." –Psalm 34:18

I launched into an indepth study and discovered three significant words that are the key to understanding this powerful verse:

1. "Broken; Contrite" The Hebrew word here is "Shabare," and it refers to something that has been crushed into small particles or ground into powder, like a rock that has been pulverized. Shabare was a pretty common word in biblical days.

The doctors knew this word because it was the word they would use when someone came to them with a severely broken and shattered bone. This is not your typical hair-line fracture. This word described a bone that had been severely shattered.

The Potters knew this word. This was the word used when a potter wasn't pleased with the vessel he was working on and so he would just crush the flawed vessel and start over making it into the beautiful vessel he wanted it to be.

The Sailors knew this word. When a ship would run aground and be broken to pieces by the relentless waves, they would use the word Shabare to describe the process of the ship being broken into pieces.

The Kings even knew this word. It was the word used to describe a kingdom when it had had been destroyed and reduced to nothing.

This is the picture of a man or woman who is broken. They feel crushed. They feel broken up. They feel reduced to nothing.

What is it that God wants to break in us? Not our spirit, or who we are as a person. But our self-will. Our independent spirit. Our pride.

In brokenness, God is actively working to break us in the area of pride, self-will, and ego.

To be broken is to be brought low, to have no pride, no arrogance, no self-will. It is the stripping of self-reliance. The broken person knows he cannot function in any way without God. He recognizes his utter dependence upon God. The broken person has no confidence in his own righteousness or his own works, or his own ability to do anything; but he is cast in total dependence upon the grace of God working in and through him.

Brokenness is "roof off, walls down." Norman Grubb once said, *"Our lives are like a house with a roof and walls. For our hearts to be revived, the roof must come off (brokenness toward God), and the walls must come down (brokenness toward man).*

Before a man is broken, he may have been a rising superstar. But now he just sees himself as a speck of dust.

Before a man is broken, he may have loved the spotlight. But now, he loves the carpet. He just wants to lay prostrate before God and put his face in the carpet.

Before a man is broken, he may have been loud and obnoxious. He was always the life of the party. But now, he has more of a quiet, humble spirit.

Before a man is broken, he may have been quick to defend himself. But now he is quick to "agree with his adversary."

Before a man is broken, he may have been a braggart. But now he just points people to Christ.

Before a man is broken, he may have sought self-glory. But now, he only seeks God's glory.

2. "Nigh" This is perhaps the key word to unlocking the power of this verse. Most translations translate this word as "near." And at first glance, that seems to be a good translation, but as I studied this word, I saw one insight that changed the whole verse for me. The word translated "nigh" or "near" is a causative adjective meaning "*to cause* to be near." God is *caused* to be near one who has a broken heart. Something acts upon Him and draws Him to it. That something is brokenness. It is as though He is drawn to, or attracted to, or magnetized to one who is broken. Now that is different than just saying He is near. The brokenness that we go through is so beautiful and pleasing to God that He finds himself actually drawn to us at that moment! This is huge! What a beautiful thought! The very thing that makes us feel that we are repugnant to God is actually beautiful and attractive in His eyes!

At the moment I saw that, my heart leaped. All the time I was in that closet, the devil had been whispering to me things like, *"You're such a failure. Just look at what a mess you have made. God is disgusted with you. You don't deserve to be forgiven. God is sick of you. He doesn't even want to talk to You. You have ruined everything. You pathetic wretch. God won't even look at you, you're so putrid and sickening to Him. He is done with you."* And because, humanly speaking, I felt deserving of all those words, the emotion of feeling such failure and despair had caused a brokenness in my heart that I had never experienced before.

Then suddenly, the Word of God broke through like a light shining in the darkness and I realized that at the very time I was feeling all those things and Satan was filling my head with all that guilt and rejection, from God's perspective, I had never been more beautiful to Him in my entire life! All that Satan had been telling me was a lie! Of course it was! He is not capable of telling the truth. Jesus made that clear when He said in John 8:44 that Satan was...

> *" a murderer from the beginning, and does not stand in the truth, because there is no truth in him. When he speaks a lie, he speaks from his own resources, for he is a liar and the father of it."*

God was not only with me, but He *wanted* to be with me. In spite of my sin and failure, He couldn't help Himself. He is so attracted to a spirit of brokenness, that He is "caused to be near me." It's as though God is looking at a crowd of 1,000 people, and He sees just one broken person in that crowd, He smiles and says, "That's the one I want to be closest to." That is the word, "nigh." Hallelujah!

3. "Saveth" This is not the word for salvation that we use when we are talking about "being saved," or "born again." This word is very powerful. It is "save" in the sense of "rescue." God "rescues" us from our situation. This word denotes *"The removal of the present misery and the restoration of the former happiness."* Think about that for a minute. My friend, does that not spell hope with a capital "H"? There is tremendous hope in brokenness!

So, according to God's Word, I wasn't washed up. And God wasn't through with me, nor was He sick of me. He loved me! He wanted to spend time with me! He actually found me very appealing at that time! God was breaking me in order to "take the me out of me." That's the beauty of brokenness. God does His work of brokenness in our lives, and then uses us in a more pure and powerful way than ever before! Psalm 147:3 puts it this way: *"He heals the broken in heart, and binds up their wounds."*

When we turn to God with a broken and contrite heart, we discover that God's grace is magnificent and that He is willing to forgive us and use us as never before. I believe that God so highly prizes this quality of brokenness, that from the moment a person believes on Christ and is born again, God begins him on a journey to brokenness. He has to come to the end of Himself. That's why God can only use broken vessels.

And therein lies the problem. See, in our culture we are obsessed with being whole; being happy; and feeling good about ourselves. And that's how most of us view the Christian life.

We want a "painless Pentecost."

We want a "Laughing Revival."

We want Christianity "lite."

We want Hot Tub Christianity with lots of warm fuzzies.

We want gain without pain, and a resurrection without a crucifixion.

We want a crown without going by way of the cross.

Hakuna Matata. "No worries. No troubles."

But it just doesn't work that way. Because God is all about Brokenness. He is all about breaking our pride and self-will, so that the life of Christ that is on the inside can flow freely from us. Let's face it, we really have nothing of eternal value to offer anyone else except the life of Christ within us!

That is why as great a preacher as John the Baptist was, he would say, *"He must increase, but I must decrease."*

That's why the Apostle Paul would say in Philippians 1:20, 21,

> *According to my earnest expectation and my hope that in nothing I should be ashamed, but with all boldness, as always, so now also, Christ shall be magnified in my body, whether by life or by death. For to me, to live is Christ, and to die is gain.*

Paul had come to such a place of brokenness in his life that he could say, " It really doesn't matter to me whether I live or die, so long as God is being magnified in my body. If I live, it is all about Christ. And if I die, well, that is gain for me because I get to go be with Him. Paul was saying in essence,

"I have no life except His life in me."

"I have no vision, except His vision for my life."

"I have no purpose, except His purpose."

" I have no will of my own, other than His will in my life."

"For to me to live *is* Christ. And to die is gain."

That is brokenness. For the riches of the life of Christ within us to be released into the world, we must be broken and die to self.

Like Mary's alabaster box in Matthew 26:1-16. The fragrance of the expensive perfume couldn't be released until the alabaster box was broken. And when it was broken, the wonderful fragrance filled the room and blessed all who were there. As long as it remained unbroken, no one was blessed by the sweet fragrance of what was on the inside. But once it was broken, everyone was blessed by it.

Like a grain of wheat John talked about in John 12:24. The life is in the germ of wheat inside the husk. Until that seed is placed in the ground and the husk is broken, no fruit can be harvested. But when the seed is placed in the ground, and through the pressure of the dirt, wind, rain and sunshine, the outer shell is broken open, then the life-giving seed on the inside can burst forth and bring fruit.

Like Gideon's broken pitchers mentioned in Judges 7:20. The light was hidden on the inside of the pitcher. But when the order was given for the pitchers to be broken, then the light could shine forth and the victory was won.

Like the Treasure in earthen vessels mentioned by Paul in 2 Corinthians 4:7. The earthen vessels have to be broken in order for the life within to be released into the world.

Like the breaking up of fallow ground Hosea mentioned in Hosea 10:12. The hard ground has to be broken up in order for the seed to be able to grow and produce fruit.

Like the broken body of Jesus Christ on the cross in I Cor. 11:24. His body had to be broken for the life giving power of His sacrifice to be able to save us from our sins.

This is the paradox of brokenness. Life comes out of death. Victory comes by way of surrender. The way up is down! Joy comes out of sorrow. And we will never meet God in revival until we meet Him in brokenness! Our families will never be whole until husbands and wives, mamas and daddies, and young people have been broken. Our churches will never be what God intended them to be until we, the members and the pastors, have experienced brokenness.

God will only meet us at the point of brokenness. He dwells with those; that is, He is at home with those, who have a broken and contrite spirit. Nothing attracts God like brokenness, and nothing repels God like pride. And it is through brokenness that the power of God is released into our lives and into our churches.

Michael Catt said it this way: *"The message of brokenness, repentance, and revival is the 'lost' message of the church. The things that Manley Beasley, Ron Dunn, Vance Havner, Leonard Ravenhill, Bertha Smith, and others preached is now pushed aside so that we can be* 'cute and cutting edge.' *Nothing is more cutting edge than calling God's people into a right relationship with Christ!*

When Paul wrote to the Corinthians, they were impressed with orators who could bewitch them and hold them under their influence by their persuasive words. Paul came and preached the foolishness of the Cross! He said, "I determined not to know anything among you save Jesus Christ and Him crucified!"

It's not about the messenger. It's not about the methods. It is the message that counts. We've fallen pray to the gods of church growth, image, success, and a thousand other idols paraded around like a golden calf. We call it 'god', but it's a long way from the Scriptures. We've added stuff, technology, and systems (which are not bad), but we've neglected sanctification, truth, and repentance. We have programs, but lack power. We have events, but our evangelism leaves much to be desired. We pray, but where is the unexplained power of God in our services?"

Oh! We need a baptism of tears today! We need to cry out to God for a spirit of brokenness!

Jeremiah said, "Oh, that my head were waters!"

The Psalmist said, "Rivers run down my eyes continually!"

Charles Finney said, "We will not see revival in the church until Mr. Amen and Mr. Wet Eye come back to church."

But our eyes are dry because our hearts are dry!

Revival comes when there is a deep conviction of sin that leads to repentance, followed by a spirit of brokenness and humility.

I have a great appreciation for Claude King who, along with Henry Blackaby, wrote *Experiencing God*, and who has a deep burden for revival in our nation. In a phone conversation with me in 2020, Claude shared the following insight on revival:

"In the prelude to the Great Prayer Revival of 1857-58, the New York Presbyterian Synod's call to prayer following the financial collapse in 1857 said this:

"In view of the recent commercial disaster that has come upon our country, the Synod of New York, deeply impressed by the fact that **the Lord has a controversy with His people,** *and that it is incumbent on them to humble themselves beneath His hand, does solemnly recommend to all its churches to set apart _____ as a day of special humiliation and prayer to Almighty God that He will have mercy upon us."*

I believe we need to ask God this question: *"Lord, do you have a controversy with Your people?"* If He does, then we need to make haste to get to the altars in humility, brokenness, and repentance before it is too late."

We need to hear once again the famous words of Abraham Lincoln in The National Proclamation for a Day of Fasting on April 30, 1863:

"We have been preserved, these many years, in peace and prosperity. We have grown in numbers, wealth and power as no other nation has ever grown. But we have forgotten God. We have forgotten the gracious hand which preserved us in peace, and multiplied and enriched and strengthened us; and we have vainly imagined, in the deceitfulness of our hearts that all these blessings were produced by some superior wisdom and virtue of our own. Intoxicated with unbroken success, we have become too self-sufficient to feel the necessity of redeeming and preserving grace, too proud to pray to the God that made us!

It behooves us, then, to humble ourselves before the offended Power, to confess our national sins, and to pray for clemency and forgiveness."

That is the answer for America.

That is the answer for the church.

That is the answer for your life and mine.

Brokenness and humility before God. Confession and repentance of sin that flows out of deep conviction by the Holy Spirit.

Will it work? I think we are out of options, don't you? If, indeed, God is our only hope, then why not throw ourselves on the altar of mercy and cry out to Him for revival?

A couple of Salvation Army officers in the early days of the Salvation Army were struggling on their field of service. They wrote to William Booth, founder of the Salvation Army, and said, "We've tried everything and nothing works." He wrote back two words: "Try tears." They did. And revival came.

May it be so in our day! May it be so!

6

CHARACTERISTIC # 3
RECONCILIATION

RESTORATION AND RECONCILIATION WITHIN THE BODY OF BELIEVERS

"The unforgiving are unforgiven because they are unforgivable."
--Dr. Tom Eliff

When genuine revival comes, it will always be accompanied by deliberate acts of reconciliation and restitution between brothers and sisters in the Lord. People will no longer be content to let "bygones be bygones" and there will be a God-given zeal to obtain a clear conscience with God and with one another.

Do you know what it means to have a clear conscience? Many years ago I learned a great definition of a clear conscience. A clear conscience means that there is no unconfessed sin my life; nothing between me and God, and that there is no one anywhere who can point a finger at me and say, "You offended me, and haven't asked my forgiveness." That is a clear conscience.

Notice that a clear conscience isn't defined as not ever having offended someone. The fact is we all do that. We all get offended at times and we all offend others at times, whether we intend to or not. That I've possibly offended someone is not the issue. The issue is what do I do when I learn that I have offended someone? Do I ignore it? Do I downplay it? Do I pretend it never happened? Do I tell the other person that they shouldn't be so sensitive and touchy? Do I make excuses?

Scripture makes it clear that when I am the offended one, I am simply to forgive the offender by the grace of God. The fact is, hurts come in many packages. There are physical hurts, emotional hurts, verbal hurts, all kinds of hurts. We have all experienced pain at the hands of someone else, and sometimes at the hand of those who are closest to us.

But when I have been hurt, I must learn to forgive. That's what it means to be like Jesus. I am to forgive, as I have been forgiven. Biblical forgiveness is not a feeling, it is an act of the will. It's like thankfulness. We are told in Scripture to "give thanks in all things," not to "feel" thankful. You do that by exercising your will in obedience to the Master. Forgiveness operates the same way. I can choose to forgive my offender, even if I don't completely feel it at the time. You may be thinking, "But isn't that being hypocritical?" No. That's being obedient to God by faith. It is an act of the will. I am to forgive totally and completely, without expecting anything in return and without holding back. I am to wipe the slate clean. I do not hold a grudge. I do not try to get even. I do not coddle anger, and I do not play the martyr. I forgive. That's what Paul means in Ephesians 4:31-32 when he says,

> *"Let all bitterness, wrath, anger, and evil-speaking be put away from you, with all malice. And be kind to one another, tenderhearted, forgiving one another, even as God in Christ forgave you."*

Someone has said that forgiveness is "giving up my right to hurt you for hurting me." Forgiveness is a deliberate decision to release a person from the debt they owe you. It is to set them free. Now why in the world would I do that? First, because you are commanded by God to do it, and if you are His child, it is non-optional. Second, because when you choose to forgive someone, it does something for them *and* for you.

What does forgiveness do for them?

It removes you as a factor in their judgment, and leaves them totally accountable to God. When you forgive, you are not letting them off the hook! You are letting them off YOUR hook, but putting them onto God's hook! The reality is, God cannot judge them until you let them out of your courtroom into His. "Vengeance is mine," says the Lord. (Romans 12:19)

So what does forgiveness do for you? A lot!

1. It releases them from *your* debt. You no longer feel that you owe them vengeance.

2. It casts you totally on the resources of God.

3. It restores you to usefulness.

4. It removes the tormentors from you (Matthew 18:32-35) Refusing to forgive someone is like drinking poison and expecting the other person to die!

5. It will remove you from the defiling root of bitterness. (Hebrews 12:15) The fruit of a tree will taste like the root it is embedded in.

That's what we're to do when we've been offended. We forgive, as we have been forgiven. But what about when we know someone out there has been offended by us? Some word we said, or some thing we did hurt their feelings, or offended them, and we now have knowledge of it. What do we do? There are two verses in Matthew's gospel that clarifies that for us:

1. Matthew 18: 15-17—*"Moreover, if your brother sins against you, go and tell him his fault between you and him alone. If he hears you, you have gained your brother. But if he will not hear you, take with you one or two more,* *that by the mouth of two or three witnesses every word may be established. And if he refuses to hear them, tell it to the church. But if he refuses even to hear the church, let him be to you like a heathen and a tax collector."*

This is Jesus' counsel. It is the best advice ever given on how to restore a broken relationship. No counselor, lawyer, or psychologist has ever improved on this counsel. I have seen this work throughout my 45 years of ministry. And notice what we are to do to the heathen, tax collectors and our enemies. We are to love them, and pray for them. (Matthew 5:44)

2. Matthew 5:23-24—*"Therefore if you bring your gift to the altar, and there remember that your brother has something against you, leave your gift there before the altar, and go your way. First, be reconciled to your brother, and then come and offer your gift."*

If you read this verse carefully, it is telling us that our worship ("your gift") is in vain, if our fellowship with our brother is not right. We are to leave our gift on the altar and quickly go and make things right with our brother, and then come back and offer our gift. This puts fellowship with our brothers and sisters ahead of our worship of the Lord. John has something to say about this in I John 4:20-21:

"If someone says "I love God," and hates his brother, he is a liar; for he who does not love his brother whom he has seen, how can he love God whom he has not seen? And this commandment we have from Him: that he who loves God must love his brother also."

If churches across this land would simply take these verses seriously and begin to practice what Jesus and John are teaching us here, we might find ourselves in revival just from these three verses!

There was a time in my life when God was teaching me the importance of humility and having a clear conscience. I didn't think at the time that there was any unfinished business that I needed to take care of with anyone. But I hadn't really asked the Lord about it. When I did, I was shocked at how quickly and specifically He answered. I found out that the Holy Spirit is amazingly specific when it comes to sin, and He has an excellent memory! I also came to understand that time has no relevance to sin. Just because it has been 10 years since you lost your temper in a deacon's meeting, doesn't mean that God, the Holy Spirit, has forgotten about it. Sin is not dealt with until it is confessed.

When I got serious about having a clear conscience, I asked the Lord to reveal to me anyone, and I meant ANYONE, in my life – past or present—that I had offended and needed to ask forgiveness of. Immediately, names, faces, and incidents began to come to mind. I made a list and even though I knew it was going to be painful and humiliating in some cases, I purposed to go to each of them and ask their forgiveness for things I had said and done. To be perfectly honest, I didn't want to do it. The flesh recoils from this kind of thing. Pride likes being King of the Hill. But my desire to be please God outweighed my desire to save face, so I did it.

The first two on my list were those who were closest to me. My wife and my parents. When I approached them separately, and told them that God had convicted me that I had wronged them and needed to ask their forgiveness, two things happened. My heart was so tenderized toward them, that I could not hold back the tears. And they, sensing my sincerity, were quick to offer forgiveness and encouragement.

My parents were incredulous that I was confessing as far back as my teenage years having a rebellious attitude, disrespecting them at times, and being lazy around the house. The phone conversation ended with lots of tears and affirmations of love from all of us, and our relationship entered a new level of love and trust and transparency.

Then there was my former college professor. She was a liberal Episcopalian teaching in a Southern Baptist College. Frankly, I never understood that. She made statements in our classes that a couple of us ultra-conservative Baptists simply couldn't let go unchallenged. She defended Evolution. She questioned the inerrancy of the Bible. We definitely clashed on that one. It became apparent to me early on that if you were a conservative Baptist, she didn't like you. And so she definitely didn't like me. It seemed she graded my papers harshly. She was always making snide remarks to me in class. And to make matters worse, she was a devoted Ole Miss Rebel fan who hated the Alabama Crimson Tide. And I was a Crimson Tide fan. One day when she came to class on Monday after Alabama had crushed Ole Miss in a football game on Saturday, the retractable map was pulled down over the blackboard, and when she pulled it up, someone had written the score of the game on the blackboard in large numbers. She spun around, looked straight at me, and if looks could kill, I would have been dead on the spot! She blasted me for doing such a wicked thing! To this day, I have no idea who did it, but I sure got the blame for it!

I have never been so glad to finish a class as I was to finish hers. Luckily, she passed me. Now, years later, as I prayed for a clear conscience, God brought her to mind, and convicted me of my dislike and bitterness toward her. I had to call her! I found her number somehow, and even though I had long graduated from that college, I placed a call to her. I didn't know what to expect, but in my gut I knew it wouldn't be good.

"Hello."

"Dr. Jones?" (not her real name)

"Yes."

"Uh, Dr. Jones, this is Terry Long". (I could hear my own voice shaking) "I was a student of yours a few years ago. You may not remember me, but…"

"Terry! Of course I remember you! How good to hear from you!" How are you doing?"

"Oh, well, good! I wasn't sure you would remember me."

"Of course I do. What can I do for you?"

"Well, Dr. Jones, I have been drawing closer to God lately, and while I was praying the other day, He brought you to mind, and I was convicted of the bad attitude I had when I was in your class. I wanted to call and ask your forgiveness for being a poor student, for not giving you the respect you deserved, and for giving you a hard time in class. Do you think you can forgive me?"

There was silence for a few seconds. Then she spoke.

"Well, Terry, I don't remember any of those things you're talking about, and I don't feel like you owe me an apology. In fact, I always thought of you as one of my best students! I loved teaching you, and enjoyed our classes so much!"

"Really? Wow. I guess I thought you didn't like me too much and I could have done much better as a student. "

"Terry, you were a very good student. I enjoyed teaching you and I'm really proud of you for going on with your education, and if you need to hear me say it, then I forgive you, but I really don't think there is anything to forgive. It was so good to hear from you!"

I can't describe the relief I felt hearing those words from a lady who I thought, or should I say, the devil had been telling me for years, couldn't stand me. That went so much better than I thought it would, and after making a few more calls to people God led me to put on my list, I was down to the last one. And this one was the one I was most anxious about.

His name was Rick Fisher. He was the chairman of deacons in the first church I served in a full time position. I was the Associate Pastor in charge of youth and children ministries. I had just gotten married, and we had moved our mobile home onto the property of the church. My total salary was $125 per week, and we squeaked by on faith, love, and a lot of peanut butter and jelly sandwiches. After almost a year on the field, in a deacon's meeting one Sunday afternoon, the subject of my financial needs came up. Bro. Rick asked me why I hadn't gotten a second job to support my needs. I told him it was because when I was hired, I was told I was full time and that I couldn't have a second job. He denied that I was full time and asked who told me that. I looked straight at the pastor, because he was the one who had told me that, and he shrugged his shoulders and said, "Don't put that monkey on my back! I never told you that." In fact, when this pastor had called me over a year earlier, the very first question I asked him was, "Is this a full time position?" He said, "Yes, it is." And proceeded to describe what all I would be doing in this 'full time job."

I had a job at a shipyard at the time, and knew that I would have to quit my job in order to take a full time position with the church. I had done that, and had never complained about trying to support my family on $125 a week. Now I was being told that no one but the pastor and me had viewed this as a full time position, and he was straight up denying it! I became upset and said some things to the Chairman of deacons in anger. From that point on, he took an adversarial position to me. Within a few months, another church called me in the same position, and I left to take that position. Now, seven years later, I was going to have to call this deacon and ask his forgiveness.

In I Timothy 5:1, Paul exhorts young Timothy, *"Do not rebuke an older man, but exhort him as a father…"*

This was what the Holy Spirit convicted me of. I knew I would never have spoken to my father the way I spoke to that deacon in that meeting. I had violated that verse in that deacon's meeting, and had carried harsh feelings toward Rick Fisher ever since. I was always fearful that if I would ever see him in public, he would say something hurtful and embarrassing. For years, I could not pass his house without fearing that he would be out in his yard and he might see me. I felt like looking the other way, but couldn't not look to see if he was there. He never was. But I couldn't shake the feeling that this man hated the very mention of my name.

It took a lot of praying to work up the courage to place that call. But I did.

"Hello."

"Bro. Rick?"

"Yes?"

I took a deep breath.

"Brother Rick, this is Terry Long." (I could envision his face turning red and him saying, "Well it's about time, you scoundrel!") He didn't.

"Brother Terry! How in the world are you doing? My wife and I were talking about you just the other day. We pray for you every day! I have been following your ministry all these years, and we are so proud to hear all that God is doing through your life!"

You could have knocked me over with a feather.

I told him why I was calling and he laughed at the idea that I had offended him. Like my college professor, he was so complimentary, and had no idea I thought he didn't like me. He told me he loved me! I was moved to tears, and realized that I had let Satan lie to me and rob me of peace about our relationship for seven long years! I was furious at Satan and at myself for listen to his lies.

Rick Fisher didn't hate me. He loved me. He and his wife had been praying for me for years. And I remembered that Satan's name means "Accuser." He is the "Accuser of the Brethren." And he had been accusing Rick Fisher to me for years. And it was all a satanic lie. But here's the thing: I would never have known that, had I not been willing to place that call to clear my own conscience. God is really, really smart!

This is why it is so important to obtain a clear conscience! This is why the Apostle Paul said in **Acts 24:16:**

> *"...I myself always strive to have a conscience without offense toward God and men."*

With each person I contacted to ask their forgiveness, it felt like a cable that had been holding me down was cut in two. Like a buoy in the ocean that is held down by underwater cables, each time I humbled myself and asked forgiveness, it felt like one of those cables was cut loose and I experienced a little more freedom. When I completed my list with Rick Fisher being the last one, I experienced incredible freedom and joy like I had never known before! That is the power of a clear conscience.

Through the years I have learned that it is important to think through your wording when attempting to obtain a clear conscience with someone you have offended. One great example in the Bible that helps us know how to approach someone we have offended is the story of the prodigal son in Luke 15:18. He had a humble, repentant spirit, carefully prepared his wording, and went to his father in person. God so honored his spirit of humility and desire to obtain a clear conscience, that he never even got a word of his confession out before his father smothered him with kisses of forgiveness. How wonderful!

Here are a few tips to consider when contemplating clearing your conscience with someone:

1. Don't say, "If I was wrong…" That projects pride, and sends the message that you aren't really convinced you did anything wrong at all.

2. Don't say, "We were both wrong." That projects blame.

3. Don't say, "I was just having a bad day. I was stressed. I needed to blow off some steam." That is justifying what you did.

4. Don't say, "I'm sorry you were offended." That says you really don't think you did anything wrong, the other person is just too sensitive.

5. Don't say, "I'm sorry." That doesn't go far enough.

6. It's better to say, "I was wrong." Or, "God has shown me that I wronged you by…," Or even better, " I don't deserve your forgiveness, but could you ever find it in your heart to forgive me?" That hits the nail on the head.

7. Don't *expect* forgiveness, *plead* for it.

8. Remember this rule of thumb when it comes to confession: Let the circle of confession be as broad as the circle of offense. If you sinned privately, confess it to God and go on. If you sinned in front of your wife and children, confess it to God and get right with your wife and children. If you sinned in front of a small group, confess it to God and get right with the small group. If you sinned in front of the church, confess it to God and get right with the church. Keep the circle of confession limited to the circle of offense.

9. Never give the gory details of sin. Be discreet with your confession. It is never right to paint sinful images in the minds of other people with your confession. Keep it simple and discreet.

As we have learned in recent days from the political arena, "Words matter." Don't let your good intentions be ruined by poorly prepared wording.

You may say, "But what if they refuse to forgive?" If you genuinely and humbly ask forgiveness, it's important to understand that whether they forgive you or not in that moment, once you've confessed and asked their forgiveness, your conscience is clear. Immediately. You can walk away with a clear conscience. If they refuse to forgive you, then that becomes a problem between them and God.

Your conscience being clear is not dependent upon the other person granting forgiveness. Asking forgiveness is your part; Granting forgiveness is their part. Your conscience is clear the moment you ask forgiveness. If they refuse, then the problem is on their shoulders, and you free God up to deal with them. At any rate, you must keep in mind that your ultimate goal is not to secure their forgiveness, but to obtain a clear conscience. That has been done once you have acknowledged your wrong and asked for forgiveness. Remember that forgiveness is only a beginning. Sometimes it takes time to rebuild trust. Forgiveness and trust are two different things. Forgiveness can be granted immediately, but it takes time and effort to rebuild trust and relationships.

There are only a handful of reasons why a person might refuse to forgive:

1. Their balance is upset. (Picture a set of scales; balances) On one side is guilt and on the other side is blame. They may choose not to forgive because they know that they also are guilty of some wrong, but they've been balancing their own guilt by blaming you for your sin, and if they were to free you of blame by forgiving, then that leaves them with their guilt and nothing to balance it with. So, they may be hesitant to grant forgiveness.

2. They don't sense genuine repentance.

3. They want to see some evidence of change in you first.

4. They expect restitution, rather than words.

5. They need time to heal.

These are the main reasons people will not forgive. At any rate, you can go away rejoicing that you have done the right thing, and continue to pray for God to grant them the grace to forgive.

"But what if the person I offended is deceased?" In that case, you can ask God's forgiveness, and if others were directly affected, you can go to them, or to the nearest of kin, if God leads you to do so.

"But what if the offense occurred before salvation?" You must still clear the offense. Salvation takes care of the sin, but there are sometimes consequences of the sin that must be dealt with. This can become one of the most powerful testimonies of a changed life by Christ!

"Should I do it by letter, by email, over the phone, or in person?" It is my belief that it should not be done by letter or email or text. This provides documentation; a record of the sin, and the whole point is erasing the sin through confession and forgiveness. The best way to obtain a clear conscience with a person is in person, where they can see the look of remorse on your face, and hear the grief in your words. A phone call can be effective for the same reason, if seeing them in person is not possible. But not a letter, not an email, and not a text.

I won't lie. It is tough to say, "I am so sorry. I was wrong. Can you find it in your heart to forgive me?" But when true revival comes, you will want to get right with that person you have had the falling out with. You will want to pay that debt you owe. You will want to forgive the one who has hurt you and you will want to ask forgiveness of the ones you have hurt.

When genuine revival comes, men and women in the church are going to be led by the Holy Spirit to get right with one another. Again, this is why evangelism is *down* the aisle, but revival is *across* the aisle.

The power of the early church is revealed in the repetition of this one phrase: *"They were of one mind and in one accord."* Over and over that phrase is repeated in the Book of Acts. They were truly united. Now compare that with the modern day church. There is so much bitterness and unforgiveness in the church today that it is amazing that anyone ever gets saved. Backbiting, gossip and slander pervades the church. We make jokes about it, but it is no laughing matter. And Facebook is no friend to church and relationships! I believe some churches would experience revival if their members cancelled their facebook accounts! No wonder we can't feel the Holy Spirit in our midst!

Someone has said, "The church is a lot like Noah's ark. If it weren't for the storm on the outside, we couldn't stand the stench on the inside."

> "To dwell above with the saints we love,
> Oh, that will be glory!
> But to dwell below with the saints we know,
> Well, that's a different story!"

I heard a story about a man who chartered a deep sea fishing boat. He couldn't swim. At some point in the day, he fell overboard. As he was flailing around in the water, the Captain reached down and grabbed his arm, but the arm came off! It was a prosthetic arm. Then the Captain grabbed him by the leg, but it came off too. It was a prosthetic leg! The man continued to flail in the water and the Captain grabbed him by the hair, but his hair came off. It was a toupee. By this time, the flustered Captain yelled to the man, "Mister, if you don't stick together, there's no way I can save you!"

The church is a lot like that. If we don't stick together, we will never get anywhere!

I like to think of the church as the wheel of a bicycle. Jesus is the hub; the center; the foundation, and we, the members, are the individual spokes of the wheel. The further away from the hub we get, the further away from each other we get also. But as each of us begins to move closer to the hub, guess what? We get closer to each other too. The spokes of a bicycle wheel are closest to each other when they are closest to the hub.

A.W. Tozer understood this. He said:

> *Has it ever occurred to you that one hundred pianos all tuned to the same fork are automatically tuned to each other? They are of one accord by being tuned, not to each other, but to another standard to which each one must individually bow. So one hundred worshippers meeting together, each one looking away to Christ, are in heart hearer to each other than they could possibly be, were they to become "unity" conscious and turn their eyes away from God to strive for closer fellowship."*

In one church I pastored, there was a family that had at one time been prominent and active in the church. For the first year I was there, although the father came and sang in the choir, his wife and kids never came. From time to time someone would mention her name and say how they missed her and wished she would come back to church. One day I asked someone why this mother had quit coming to church. They told me that she had been caught having an affair with the husband of the church pianist, who happened to be her best friend, and it became a major scandal in the church. As most churches tend to do, this scandal was simply swept under the rug and forgotten about. But it was obvious to me, that the church still loved this woman and missed her. The problem was no one knew what to do about it.

One day I made an appointment to visit with this lady and made sure there was someone else there when I did. All three of her kids were there. As I talked to her, she shared with me how ashamed she was of what she had done. She told me that she had asked God to forgive her and He had. She asked her husband and children to forgive her and they had graciously forgiven her. She had also asked the church pianist to forgive her, and she had said she forgave her. As you might imagine, their friendship was greatly damaged when this happened, and now they hardly spoke to each other. But she told me that when she had tried to come back to church and sit in the very back, she couldn't help but feel like the people were judging her and looking down on her. So she decided not to come back to church at all.

Her tears flowed freely and her pain and embarrassment was evident as she talked about how much she missed her church and her friends. I asked her if she had ever thought about asking forgiveness from the whole church, since this sin had become a public matter. She looked surprised, and said, "Oh, I could never do that." But I showed her that she had already asked everyone's forgiveness that she loved and they had granted it freely. Only one thing remained, and that was to ask the church for forgiveness. I told her to pray about it for a couple of weeks, had prayer with her and her kids and left. Two weeks later she showed up on a Sunday morning and sat in the back. After I had preached, much to everyone's surprise, she was the first one down the aisle. Weeping, she told me she was ready to ask forgiveness from the church and asked if I would stand on the platform with her. I said I would, and so we stopped the music and walked up on the platform together. I told the church that she had something to say. She said, "Everyone here knows my sin. Everyone here knows how I hurt the people I love and those who were closest to me by sinning the way I did. I have asked all of them to forgive me, and they have. I have asked God to forgive me and He has. I have asked my husband and children to forgive me and they have. But the one thing I now realize that I failed to do is to ask you, my church family, to forgive me. Will you forgive me for what I have done?" It was short, heartfelt, and discreet.

As soon as she asked the question, I spontaneously turned to the chairman of the deacons who was in the choir, and said, "Mr. Chairman of deacons, this lady has asked forgiveness from the church for her offense. What do the deacons say?" With no preparation, he stood and responded with one powerful word. **"Forgiven!"** Picking up the cue, the deacons all stood and said in unison, **"Forgiven!"** I then turned back to the church body. There were about 350 people present that day, and I said, "Church, you have just heard this dear lady's confession and she has asked your forgiveness. What says the church?" And almost unanimously, the church said that one powerful word, **"Forgiven!"**

Immediately, the sweet dove of the Holy Spirit descended upon that place, and God began to move on people's hearts. The lady was crying, I was crying, the deacons were crying, and most of the congregation was crying. For a moment, it seemed time stood still. Suddenly, the pianist, who was once her best friend, and whose husband she had had the affair with, stood up from the piano, ran across the platform and threw her arms around her former best friend, and they stood there hugging and crying for several minutes. Heaven came down.

Something broke in the atmosphere over the church that day, and the fire of the Holy Spirit fell. People spontaneously began coming down the aisle and getting on their knees at the altar and weeping before the Lord. Someone stood up and said, "Bro. Terry, I need to get something right with God and this congregation." Then someone else, and then someone else. This went on right past twelve noon. That service lasted until 2:30 in the afternoon. Revival came and we began to see souls saved in an unprecedented manner in our church. That year, we led our Association in baptisms, and half of the reported baptisms for all 44 churches were from our church.

That is what happens when reconciliation and restoration takes place in a church. If you don't believe that this subject of reconciliation and forgiveness is on the heart of God, consider this "coincidence." As I was in the middle of writing this chapter, just yesterday I received an email from Dr. Ronnie Floyd, past President of the Southern Baptist Convention and current President of the SBC Executive Committee. The title of the article is this:

"Unforgiveness is the #1 obstacle to the power of God in our lives, marriages, churches, denominations, and even nations."

That was no coincidence! God was affirming the truth of this chapter! Here is what Dr. Floyd said in part in this powerful article:

"I believe unforgiveness is the #1 obstacle to the next great release of God's power in a person's life, marriage, church, denomination, and even in a nation. Every person has been affected by unforgiveness in one way or another. Perhaps someone has offended us, said something untrue about us, or even intentionally tried to hurt us and destroy our reputation. This may have led to holding a grudge or having deep-rooted bitterness toward them.

Sometimes when relationships go south, forgiveness is refused. As we know, churches, denominations, and personal friendships can be ruptured by the wounds of unforgiveness and bitterness. Hurt people often hurt people.

God freely and sacrificially forgives us; therefore, we should forgive others. Friends, never let anyone outside of your circle of love. Forgiveness is imperative in the life of a Christ follower. Therefore we, who are forgiven for our own sins, must choose to forgive others.

Refuse all unforgiveness. When unforgiveness prevails, broken relationships will always follow. The power of God is never placed upon a person, a marriage, a family, a church, a denomination, or a nation when unforgiveness prevails. This is also true for Christian leaders.

If your anger is raging and your criticism about others is unceasing, you are choosing to live with unforgiveness and, at the same time, choosing to live without the power of God upon you. Forgiveness is the better way. Yes, complete forgiveness. Forgiveness is God's way. This always leads to experiencing the power of God and the blessings that come from the presence of the Lord."

Indeed, when there is an outpouring of the Holy Spirit in genuine revival, it will be accompanied by restoration, reconciliation, and forgiveness in the body of Christ.

7

CHARACTERISTIC # 4 JOY

A NEW AND UNBRIDLED SENSE OF JOY AND FREEDOM

"Joy is the flag flown from the castle of the heart when the King is enthroned." -
-Dr. Jack Taylor

"There is more joy in Jesus in 24 hours than there is in the world in 365 days. I have tried them both!
--R.A. Torrey

The Bible has a lot to say about joy. But what exactly is joy? One lady defined it this way: "Joy is seeing your husband's old girlfriend, and she's fatter than you!" Now that may bring a momentary sense of satisfaction, but I doubt that is real joy. I like Jack Taylor's definition given above. "Joy is the flag flown from the castle of the heart when the King is enthroned." Another has defined joy as "the spontaneous expression of my spirit when my soul, i.e. my mind, will, and emotions, is in fellowship with the Lord." Still another quipped, "It's easy to sing, when you walk with the King!" I like that!

I like joy, don't you? And I like being around joyful people. However, this seems to be a missing element in the lives of so many believers.

Many Christians today are a lot like Lazarus after Jesus raised him from the dead. He was alive, but still bound by grave cloths! Alive, but bound! That describes many of us today. We've been saved, but we are still bound by all kinds of sin and guilt. Bad habits, wrong thought patterns, bitterness, anger, and moral impurity form chains of sin that keep us bound to the past. Convinced by the enemy of our soul that while victory might be attainable for others, we, however, are so much weaker than others, it will never happen for us. We should just give up on the idea of having victory and joy and simply settle for fewer defeats in life. We are alive, but bound!

But here's some good news! Jesus didn't leave Lazarus in that bound condition! He gave the command, *"Unbind him, and let him go!"* And that is exactly what God does in times of revival—He breaks the chains of sin and sets us free!

Have you ever experienced the joy of being set free from the burden and guilt of sin? One well known Christian psychologist has said that over half the patients in mental institutions could walk out today if they could somehow find freedom from guilt and bitterness.

In January of 2012, I felt led to erect a 14' cross beside the road at a busy intersection in south Mississippi and go to that cross for 100 days to pray and seek God for revival. What happened in those 100 days was beyond my wildest expectations. It was the subject of my first book, *100 Days at the Cross.* Of the 1500 people who visited that cross for prayer during those life-changing days, a significant number of them came seeking relief from the burden of guilt over past sins. One of those was a man named Rodney Fernandez.

Rodney owned a muffler shop in the nearby town of Moss Point, MS. Every day on his way to work he had to pass by this cross. Rodney's life was wracked with remorse, guilt, and bitterness. But every day when he passed that cross, he felt God speaking to him. One day he made the decision that on his way to work that morning, he would stop at the cross. He sat down the night before and wrote out his burdens on several pages of notebook paper. I remember seeing his tan Toyota Tundra pull off the road, and him getting out of his truck in his muffler shop uniform. He started to walk down toward the cross, but never made it past the tailgate of his truck. He just stood there weeping. I noticed him standing there crying, and walked over to see if I could help him.

After a few minutes, he was able to recover enough of his voice to ask for a hammer and a nail to put his prayer request on the Cross. I looked down and it appeared that he was clutching a short novel written on notebook paper folded up in his hand. I handed him the hammer and a nail and stood back as he walked a few steps toward the cross. He abruptly stopped and just stood there for awhile looking up and down the cross. I wondered what he was hesitating for, but wouldn't ask. At this point in the 100 day prayer vigil, hundreds of prayer requests had been nailed to the cross. Most were from about knee-high all the way up to the cross beam, but the bottom three feet of the cross was bare. After several minutes, he turned to me with tears streaming down his face, shook his head and said, " I am not worthy to put my prayers anywhere near theirs." He slowly walked around to the backside of the cross, got down on both knees and began to sweep away the dirt from base of the cross. And that's where Rodney Fernandez nailed his request. At the base of the cross. In the dirt. On the backside of it. I remember thinking, "Lord, if I have never seen true humility in my life, I am seeing it now."

Rodney stayed on his knees in the dirt on the backside of the cross for a while praying and weeping. I could hear him murmuring his prayer. I could see him rocking back and forth on his knees and I could hear him crying out his pain to the Lord. After a while, he got up and walked over to me and handed me the hammer. I asked him if there was anything he wanted to talk about and he shook his head and said no. He said it would take too long to tell me about all the sin and shame of his life. I asked him if I could pray for him. We bowed our heads and I prayed for Rodney. When we finished, he looked up and said, "Well, maybe I can tell you a little bit of where I have been in my life." So for the next 30 minutes, he stood there and poured out his story of sin and guilt. He said he hadn't had a good night's sleep in years. I hugged his neck, assured him of God's love and marvelous forgiveness, and he left.

The next morning, that same tan Toyota Tacoma pickup pulled off the road. But this time it had hardly come to a stop when the driver side door flew open and Rodney Fernandez got out running. He ran all the way down to where I was and gave me a huge bear hug. He said, "I slept! I slept all night! It was the best sleep I've had in years! And I am free! No more guilt! God has set me free! I am so happy I don't know what to do! I thank God for you and I thank God for this cross! My life is changed!" He was literally dancing around me in a circle as he shared this amazing new joy and freedom he was experiencing. And for the rest of the time I was at the cross, Rodney's little truck would pull off the road at least three times a week and he would run down to me with a grin a mile wide and hug me and thank me for putting that cross up. I will never forget Rodney. About five years after my experience with the Cross, I was passing through Moss Point, and I spotted a building with a sign out front that said, "Fernandez Mufflers". I knew that had to be Rodney's place, so I stopped in. There was Rodney, smiling big as ever, and I noticed on the counter next to the cash register, there were Bibles, gospel tracts, and other Christian materials. Rodney was still telling people about a God who can forgive and set you free from sin and guilt!

This is one of the defining marks of genuine revival. Joy that is pure and untainted. Freedom from the chains of sin that is…well… liberating! People get set free from all kinds of junk that has wreaked havoc in their lives for years. Chains that have enslaved them to Satan and guilt and misery are suddenly broken and they get a taste of real freedom from sin, producing a joy and lightheartedness that is akin to Ebenezer Scrooge on Christmas morning when he realized he hadn't missed Christmas after all! (I always choke up when I watch that scene because it reminds me of the pure, unbridled sense of joy that comes when we realize that we've been saved!)

When the fire falls, and revival comes, the desire to be entertained and to feel good is exposed for what it really is: A cheap substitute for true godly joy. Have you ever realized that there is a very real link between genuine revival and abounding joy? David demonstrated this when he said, *"Wilt thou not revive us again, that thy people may **rejoice** in Thee? (Psalm 85:6)*

Notice that the singular stated purpose in David asking for revival was so that the people of God could truly rejoice in the Lord. Revival always results in joy. Rejoicing is the by-product of a genuine move of God in revival according to David's prayer. So the hallmark of our worship when the Holy Spirit is poured out in revival will be an unbridled sense of joy and freedom in Christ, rather than cheap, gimmicky entertainment. In revival, rather than pseudo miracles and false spirituality, the Lord Jesus Christ takes center stage as the sole object of our worship.

Do you remember what it was like when you were first saved? We were in love with Jesus! Overwhelmed with the realization of what God had done for us, our hearts were full of joy and we felt so FREE! We were so excited about reading our Bible, telling others about Jesus, and learning to pray that we didn't even need television! We were on fire for God! But sadly, today, we're not on fire for God; we barely have a little fever.

If you don't believe me, just look around at the people sitting near you the next time you are in church. Do they look happy? Are they singing their hearts out to the Lord? Or do they look like they would rather be anywhere else on the planet besides church? I agree with what one rural preacher said, "Many Christians today look like they were born on the dark side of the moon, weaned on a dill pickle, baptized in vinegar, have been sucking on green persimmons, and they walk around with their bottom lip sticking out so far they could suck a marble out of a gopher hole!" They have no joy, no peace and no victory!

Yet it was Nehemiah who said, *"The joy of the Lord is our strength!"* (Neh. 8:10) Loosely translated, "No joy=no strength." If that's the case then, we can understand why most churches don't have the power to blow the fuzz off a peanut. In truth, we are in a battle-to-the-death with the enemy of our souls, but because there is no joy in our lives, and therefore, no strength, the average Christian doesn't have the power to whip a sick rabbit, much less deal with "principalities, powers, rulers of the darkness of this world, and spiritual hosts of wickedness in heavenly places." (Eph. 6:12)

We are to live in such a way that others want what we have! Revival produces a kind of contagious joy in our life that makes our testimony of the life-changing power of Jesus Christ believable, and brings a winsomeness and magnetism to our Christian life.

I love what one new Christian said in a letter to his pastor. He said, *"I am continually amazed at the grace of God, and have grown in my love for my Savior. I cannot believe that I have been saved from what I deserved!"*

Unfortunately, too many Christians are no longer amazed at the grace of God that saved them and delivered them from the clutches of Satan. We've gotten over it. We've lost the joy of our salvation, and our faces show it.

This is what led Nietzsche to say, *"If you Christians want me to believe in your Redeemer, you're going to have to look a lot more redeemed."*

Ghandi once said, *"If Christians would really live according to the teachings of Christ, as found in the Bible, all of India would be Christian today."*

The problem is that most Christians are in a rut, spiritually. Have you ever been in a spiritual rut? I have. It's a miserable time. I hear preachers sometimes refer to lost people as living a "miserable life of sin." Well, I know some Christians who live a "miserable life of holiness." They are in a rut in their spiritual lives. Do you know what a rut is? A rut is a grave with both ends kicked out of it. It is "deadly monotony." It is "dying from sameness." It is living a life of abject boredom when you have the most exciting, dynamic person in the universe living inside you. It is a time of non-productivity; a period of ineffectiveness; nothing's happening in your life. You know you don't have it all together even though you try to project an image that you do. Your spiritual life is blah, dull, gray, neutral, and lukewarm. Your Christianity is as cold as ice, as dry as dust, as pale as a corpse, and as dead as King Tut! That's what a spiritual rut is.

I love the story of Blind Bartimaeus in Mark 10. Talk about a man in a rut! His life was one of monotonous misery! Every day was the same. Someone led him out to the roadside so he could beg for alms in hopes to get enough in his cup to buy a piece of bread. But one day Jesus of Nazareth passed by, and Bartimaeus mustered up enough courage to cry out to Jesus for mercy. And one of the sweetest verses in the Bible says, *"And Jesus stood still."* (Mark 10:49) Wow! Jesus stood still for one blind beggar. And Bartimaeus' life would never be the same. He was healed and given his eyesight, and no longer had to beg.

In the introduction to that sermon I like to make a series of statements and ask the people in the audience to fill in the blank to make sure they understand what a rut really is. Let's see if you can do it:

A. *I'm ready to throw in the* _____.

B. *I feel like resigning from the human* _____.

C. *I'm at the end of my* _____.

D. *I'm just a bundle of* _____.

E. *My life is falling* _____-.

F. *I'm at my wit's* _____.

G. *Things just can't get any* _____.

H. *I'm hanging on by a* _____.

. . .

Answers: A. Towel B. Race. C. Rope D. Nerves E. Apart F. End G. Worse H. Thread

So how did you do? Most people can fill in every blank. They get an A+ in Rutology. We've all been there. Many of us are there now. And it's because we're not hearing a fresh word from God in our daily lives, we've drifted spiritually away from God, and we've lost the joy of our salvation. We need Revival because our hearts have grown cold and our lives are in a rut.

Did you know that God *commanded* the Fathers in Deuteronomy 16, Exodus 23:17 and 34:23 to take their families three times a year to Jerusalem. Why? To get out of the normal routine so they can hear a fresh word from God. This was a time of great celebration, feasting and worship. It was the highlight of their year, three times a year. It was a time of great joy and gladness. And it broke up the monotony of everyday life and refocused their attention on God. It brought the joy back into their lives. Pastors who like to boast that they haven't taken a vacation in three years (as if that is some kind of sign of spiritual maturity and dedication), need to go back and meditate on that passage of Scripture! It is not a sin to take a vacation, enjoy time off with your family, and smile a little bit, and just be normal!

That's one reason why I love the Apostle Paul. He wrote more about joy and rejoicing in the Christian life than any other New Testament writer, and bear in mind that he wasn't writing from a beautiful vacation spot on a beach in the Bahamas. No sir! Most of the time he was writing from a prison cell or a dungeon. Yet, listen to his words on joy:

> *"Rejoice in the Lord always, and again I say, rejoice!"* (Phil. 4:40

> *"Finally, my brethren, rejoice in the Lord."* (Phil. 3:1)

> *"Rejoice always!"* (I Thess. 5:16)

> *"...as sorrowful, yet always rejoicing..."* (2 Cor. 6:10)

> *"Yes, and if I am being poured out as a drink offering on the sacrifice and service of your faith, I am glad and rejoice with you all."* (Phil. 2:17)

In the spring of 2020 I read through the Bible in 90 days and marked every reference to the blood and to Atonement. (About 460 times) It was such a profitable exercise that I decided to do it again in the fall, but this time I marked every reference to joy, gladness, happiness and rejoicing. Do you know what I discovered as I marked over 572 references to joy and happiness? Our God is a happy God who wants his people to be happy, joy-filled people living out their Christian lives in the power of the Holy Spirit.

Once I marked every verse that mentioned joy, happiness, gladness, or rejoicing I became amazed at how the subject of joy permeates the Scriptures! Every time I open my Bible now I see passages about joy! They are everywhere! But most Christians aren't experiencing this joy because they have allowed Satan, sin, and sourpuss Christians to cast a pall of gloom over their lives and rob them of this God-given fruit of the Spirit called joy!

They have been in a rut for so long, they're singing Hee Haw's famous theme song of *"Gloom, despair, and agony on me; Deep dark depression, excessive misery. If it weren't for bad luck I'd have no luck at all. Gloom, despair, and agony on me."*

They are in dire need of a personal revival. They may not show it on the outside, but on the inside they are dying every day.

When David sinned against God with Bathsheba, he lost the joy of his salvation. He prayed in Psalm 51:12, *"Restore to me the joy of thy salvation"*... Have we forgotten the sheer joy of walking with Jesus in the power of the Holy Spirit? Have we gotten too busy to spend time in His presence every day? Do we remember how wonderful it felt to be saved? I mean, when was the last time you just sat down and gave some serious thought to what it really means to be saved? "God, I don't want to ask you for anything today. I just want to thank you from the bottom of my heart for saving my soul. God, if you never did anything else for me this side of Heaven, that would be enough to praise you for all eternity! We need to be like the guy who was asked if he was sure he was saved and he said, *"I'm so saved I could swing over Hell on a rotten cornstalk singing Amazing Grace How Sweet the Sound!"* Now that's what I call "knowing that you know that you know you are saved!"

I remember when I was pastoring in the Mississippi Delta, and I was invited to preach in a Black church for their Regional Conference. It was my first time to preach in a Black church, and I didn't know exactly what to expect. I preached a sermon on the greatness of salvation and I used an outline from an old evangelist by the name of Ed Vallowe. The outline went like this: God's salvation is the greatest thing in all the world because:

1. God thought it.

2. Jesus bought it.

3. The Holy Spirit wrought it.

4. The Bible taught it.

5. The devil fought it.

6. I caught it!

They nearly preached me to death! At first, there were seven pastors on the platform behind me. They started out on the first point saying "Amen, brother. Come on!" But by the third point, they were stomping their feet and saying, "Amen! Preach it, brother!" By the Fifth point they were on their feet clapping their hands and when I got to the last point, all Heaven broke loose! We had a happy time! I thought I was going to get raptured on the spot. A sweet little lady came up to me after the service and said, "I didn't know white preachers could whoop!" I said, "Whoop?" She said, "Yessir, whoop!" I said, "What is whooping?" She said, "It is what you were doing at the end of your sermon!" Well, I didn't know I was whooping, but I did know they got excited about salvation that night! There was joy!

And dare I say it? Critical Race Theory and Intersectionality cannot touch that kind of unity and that kind of unbridled joy! We were not "White people" and "Black people;" we were not the "oppressed" and the "oppressor" that night. We were just a bunch of blood-washed sinners saved by grace rejoicing in God our Savior!

God's people are supposed to be happy, Spirit-filled people! Not silly or shallow. Not phony. Not what one writer years ago referred to in an article in Christianity Today as "shiny, gaggy, happy," people. Have you ever been around someone like that? They walk around with a goony grin on their face all the time looking like they slept with a clothes hanger in their mouth the night before. They're so shiny, gaggy, happy, they're not real, and people just look at them and shake their head. No, that's not biblical joy. I'm talking about real joy. Contagious joy. The kind of joy that Jesus had. That Paul had.

Have you ever wondered how Paul could talk so much about joy when he spent over half of his adult life in a prison cell? Paul had something I like to call **Jailhouse Joy.**

Jailhouse Joy is that joy you can have even in the worst of circumstances. This is what enabled Paul and Silas to sing and praise God at midnight in the philippian jailer's jail, causing an earthquake to come and their bonds and chains falling off and the jailer and his family getting saved! This is what the Bible is referring to when it talks about "joy unspeakable and full of glory" and "peace that surpasses all understanding." This is what Paul is referring to when he says, "For to me, to live is Christ, and to die is gain." (Phil. 1:21) This is what led Jim Elliot, the martyred missionary to the Auca Indians, to pray, *"Forgive me, Lord, for being so ordinary while claiming to know so extraordinary a God!"*

The book of 2nd Timothy is the last letter Paul wrote just before he was martyred. It is his swan song. It is his death bed statement to his young son in the ministry, Timothy. These are Paul's last words. Now, usually death bed statements are rather somber and serious in nature. But not so with the ironclad Apostle. He said in chapter 1, verse 12,

> "...nevertheless, I am not ashamed, for I know whom I have believed and am persuaded that He is able to keep that which I have committed unto him until that day."

And in Chapter four, verse 6,

> "...the time of my departure is at hand. I have fought a good fight, I have finished my course, I have kept the faith; henceforth there is laid up for me a crown of righteousness, which the Lord, the righteous Judge, shall give me on that day, and not to me only but also to all them who love His appearing."

Paul may have been about to die, but he was still rejoicing. Still standing strong. Still unashamed. And still winning souls. He knows that in a few days his head will roll from his shoulders, but he is not bothered about it at all. He actually sounds like he is kind of looking forward to it. I think Paul had seen just enough of heaven (2 Cor. 12:1-3) to make him homesick!

I like to imagine ole Paul walking around in his cell. He has completed his three missionary journeys. His hair is a silver-gray. His skin is wrinkled. His balance is a bit unsteady. He is a little stoop-shouldered, and his eyesight has dimmed. He is in the twilight of life. The Apostle Paul is now an old man. In a few days, he will be dead. Under the command of Nero, Emperor of Rome, he will be executed. But before he dies, he has one last letter to write. He wants to write to Timothy, his young son in the ministry. He wants to encourage him not to worry. So he writes the letter we refer to as 2 Timothy. He tells him in chapter one, verse 8, "Don't be ashamed of the testimony of our Lord, nor of me his prisoner." He says, " Timothy, don't be ashamed. It's worth it, son. And don't worry about me. I'm gonna be alright! I'm going home. Timothy, they have taken everything away from me that they can take. They've taken my family, my friends, my comforts, my home, my public ministry, but there's one thing they cannot take—and that's my joy!

Timothy, I still have the victory and the joy is still bubbling! Brother, I feel like singing!

> "Some through the water, some through the flood;
> Some through the fire, but all through the blood.
> Some through great sorrow, but God gives a song;
> In the night season, and all the day long."

> "Amazing grace! How sweet the sound.
> That saved a wretch like me.
> I once was lost, but now am found,
> Was blind, but now I see."

> "There is coming a day when no heartaches shall come,
> No more clouds in the sky, No more tears to dim the eye,
> All is peace forever more, on that happy golden shore,
> What a day, glorious day that will be."

"Guard! I need to write a letter. Bring me a parchment and a quill, please. "Dear Timothy. Hallelujah! Glory to God! Don't be ashamed of the Gospel! Or of me! I'm saved! It's worth it all! Jesus is so wonderful! Uh, guard, please don't shake the chain, I'm trying to write a letter to my… Oh! I see you're crying. I'm sorry. Can I help you? What's that? Who is this Jesus I'm always talking about? You don't understand how I can be so happy? Well, let me tell you about it. You see, I was on the road to Damascus, and I met this man named Jesus…"

No wonder the historians tell us they had to change the guards on Paul every four hours. I think I know why! He was winning them to Jesus!

"Oh, joy! 2 new guards! Hey! Do you think I could get a parchment and a quill? I have a new letter to write. And while I'm writing, since we're stuck with each other for the next four hours, may I tell you about my wonderful Savior?"

Think about it. Paul is thrown in jail. Instead of whining about his situation, his Jailhouse Joy kicks in and he begins praising God and sharing the gospel with the guards who are chained to him. They get saved. Then four more are brought in and the process repeats itself. That's what I call "A Chain Reaction!"

I have often wondered this: If you were chained to the Apostle Paul for four hours a day, who do you think the real prisoner would be, you or him?

When genuine revival comes, joy and freedom are not far behind. Joy, laughter, and singing are signs that the Spirit is being poured out in genuine revival. No wonder the Psalmist said, *"When the Lord restored the fortunes of Zion, we were like those who dream. Then our mouth was filled with laughter, and our tongue with shouts of joy."* (Psalm 126:1-2)

So here is my question: How's your joy today? Do you need a dose of "Jailhouse Joy"? Why not pause right now, lay this book aside, drop to your knees and tell God that you don't want to be a joyless Christian any longer. Ask Him to restore your joy. Ask Him to reveal to you anything in your life that is stealing your joy. Confess anything He reveals to you as sin. Thank Him for his love, His grace, and His forgiveness. Then ask Him to help you look and act more redeemed so that others may believe in your Redeemer! He will hear your prayer, honor your request, and joy will be yours again! Jailhouse Joy!

8

CHARACTERISTIC # 5 LORDSHIP

A RENEWAL OF OUR FIRST LOVE FOR JESUS AND A DEEP SENSE OF HIS LORDSHIP IN OUR LIVES

"Personal revival is Jesus in you, around you, through you, under you, over you, before you, and behind you." ---Anne Graham Lotz

In my dual roles as Associational Missions Director for the Choctaw Baptist Association in Butler, Alabama and Evangelism Strategist for the Alabama Baptist State Board of Missions in Prattville, Alabama, I am privileged to preach in a different church almost every Sunday. No matter what my subject is, I always try to magnify the Lord Jesus Christ and lift Him high. Sometimes in the introduction to my message I will tell the people, "It is my privilege to attempt to overwhelm you with the majesty of Jesus Christ today. My goal is that when you leave here today you will not say, "What a sermon!" but "What a Savior!"

I want to let you know, dear reader, that in this chapter I am going to attempt to overwhelm you with the majesty of Jesus Christ because when true revival comes, Jesus Christ takes center stage and He alone gets the glory. My hope is that if nothing you have read up to this point has moved you to seek God for revival, then a clear picture of the majesty and magnificence of our great Savior might do just that. So pardon me, if in the context of revival, I brag on Jesus a bit!

Any revival that doesn't exalt Jesus Christ above all things is not a true revival. In true revival, Jesus Christ is exalted above anybody or anything else. Genuine revival is always God-initiated, Holy Spirit-led, and, most of all, Christ-centered. When the fire falls and revival comes, your relationship with Jesus Christ becomes the most precious thing in your life. Your first love returns, and Jesus becomes very, very precious to you.

In an excellent paper on the subject of revival, my good friend and mentor, Dr. Larry Holly of Beaumont, Texas reminds us of Jonathan Edwards' experience of the Lordship of Christ as recounted by Martin Lloyd Jones' essay:

> *"Once, as I rode out into the woods for my health, in 1737, having alighted from my horse in a retired place, as a manner commonly has been, to walk for divine contemplation and prayer, I had a view, that for me was extraordinary, of the glory of the Son of God, as Mediator between God and man, and His wonderful, great, full, pure and sweet grace and love, and meek and gentle condescension. This grace that appeared so calm and sweet, appeared also great above the heavens. The person of Christ appeared ineffably excellent, with an excellency great enough to swallow up all thought and competition—which continued, as near as I can judge, about an hour; which kept me the greater part of the time in a flood of tears, and weeping aloud. I felt an ardency of soul to be, what I know not otherwise how to express, emptied and annihilated; to lie in the dust, and to be full of Christ alone; to love Him with a holy and pure love; to trust in Him; to live upon Him; to serve and follow Him; and to be perfectly sanctified and made pure, with a divine and heavenly purity. I have several other times had views very much of the same nature, and which have had the same effects."*

There can simply be no revival which does not manifest itself in a deep abiding sense of the Lordship of the person of the Lord Jesus Christ and a renewed love for Him. I love what John R.W. Stott once said, *"The Cross is the blazing fire at which our love for Jesus is rekindled. But we have to get close enough for its sparks to fall on us."* In genuine revival, the sparks of the blazing fire of the Cross fall on those who are seeking God thereby rekindling their love for Him!

One of the most complimented churches of the Seven Churches of Asia Minor that Jesus addressed in the first three chapters of Revelation was the Church at Ephesus in Revelation 2:1-7. If this church existed in today's world, we would give it five stars! It might be considered a model church.

It was a hard working church. *"I know your works..."*

It was a laboring church. *"I know your labor..."*

It was a patient church. *"I know your patience..."*

It was a holy church. *"and that you cannot bear those who are evil..."*

It was a discerning church. *"You have tested those who say they are apostles and are not..."*

It was a persevering church. *"You have persevered."*

It was a tireless church. *"And have not become weary..."*

But with all this going for it, according to Jesus, it was an unacceptable church. *"But I have somewhat against you. You have left your first love."*

You see, what Jesus is teaching here is that it's not only important *what* you do for God, it's also important *why* you do it. God is not only interested in the fact that you sing on the praise team, He is interested in *why* you sing on the praise team. He is not only interested in the fact that you want to serve as a deacon; He's interested in *why* you want to serve as a deacon. You see, ministry matters, but in the Kingdom of God, motives matter too. Why? Because Jesus wants more than our works, He wants our heart.

Christianity is not about your performance. It is about your love relationship with Jesus.

That's why Paul would say things like,

> *"Though I speak with the tongues of men and of angels, but have not love, I have become sounding brass or a clanging cymbal...and though I feed the poor, and though I give my body to be burned, but have not love, it profits me nothing."* (I Corinthians 13:1,3)

In an unrevived state, it is possible to love the work of the Lord without loving the Lord of the work! We often substitute the work of our hands for relationship. But Jesus wants more than just the labor of our hands, He wants the love of our heart. The fact is, you can work for Jesus without loving Him, but you cannot love Jesus without working for Him.

For many years I wondered about the meaning of the Old Testament story of the Lost Axehead that floated in 2 Kings 6. It is a fascinating passage.

> *"And the sons of the prophets said to Elisha, 'See now, the place where we dwell with you is too small for us. Please, let us go to the Jordan, and let every man take a beam from there, and let us make there a place where we may dwell. So he answered, "Go." Then one said, "Please be content to go with your servants." And he answered, "I will go." So he went with them. And when they came to the Jordan, they cut down trees. But as one was cutting down a tree, the iron ax head fell into the water; and he cried out and said, "Alas, Master! For it was borrowed." So the man of God said," Where did it fall?" And he showed him the place. So he cut off a stick, and threw it in there; and he made the iron float. Therefore he said, "Pick it up for yourself." So he reached out his hand and took it."*

Now the interesting thing about this story is that these young preachers were doing a good thing. They were doing the right thing. They were trying to make progress. They were trying to move forward. They were building something for God. They were working really hard, and in the midst of all of their work suddenly something bad happened. The axe head flew off the handle of one of the young men's axe and landed in the river. He lost his cutting edge! So what did he do? Did he continue trying to cut down trees with just the bare axe handle? Of course not! He knew what everyone else knows—you cannot cut down a tree if you've lost your cutting edge! How foolish it would have been for him to just continue on with his work, beating on trees with nothing but an axe handle! Yet, it seems that the church of the Lord Jesus Christ today has lost her cutting edge, and we're just going around beating on trees with bare axe handles!

When you open the your Bible and look at the church in the book of Acts, and you see the fellowship they had, the evangelistic power, the souls being saved, the miracles, and the growth, and then you look around at the church today, is it not painfully obvious that the church has lost something along the way?

Isn't it obvious that to a large extent, we are just going around beating on trees with bare axe handles? And every now and then someone will look up and realize that with all our activity; with all our religious commotion, statistics show that we are not felling trees anymore! So what do we do about it? Well, what we should do is stop working for the moment, go back to the place where we lost our axe head, and be willing to do whatever is necessary to regain our cutting edge. But that is not what we typically do in the church today. Instead, here is what we often do:

- We call for strategy conferences on how to make our axe handles more "user friendly."
- We bring in experts to help us learn how to swing our axe handles more effectively.
- We hold seminars on how to improve our swing.
- We take a census of the trees, bring in motivational speakers to motivate the wood choppers, and declare that this is National Tree Cutting Day with a goal of cutting

down 25% more trees than we did last year. With only an axe handle!
- We polish our axe handles so they look better than the axe handles of our competitors down the street.
- We preach sermons on 7 steps to more effective chopping with an axe handle.

And off to the woods we go!

But, alas, though the noise of the workmen is great, there is one thing missing—the sound of falling trees!

We have movement without might, energy without effectiveness, much doing, but little dynamic. And what we end up with is bruised hands, tired bodies, and wounded trees. This is leading to more and more people getting tired of chopping and working and now they are considering laying down the axe handle and leaving the forest for good. We are losing church members by the droves. For the past several years the Southern Baptist Convention has lost over 200,000 members a year. This past year, the SBC lost over 400,000 members. And this is the 13th consecutive year of membership decline and the biggest drop in membership in 100 years in the world's largest non-Catholic religious denomination. Something is definitely wrong.

What is missing? Why, the axe head, of course! We've lost our cutting edge! Now maybe this is a good time to ask the question: What exactly is the cutting edge? The cutting edge is the life of Jesus released into the world through you, by the power of the Holy Spirit.

> "...*Christ in you, the hope of glory.*" (Col. 1:27)

It is the life of Jesus Christ released through you by the Holy Spirit. That is the cutting edge!

Effective Christian ministry is not simply me trying to imitate Jesus Christ. It is not me attempting to do something for Jesus. It is me dying to self, and allowing Christ to work in and through me! It is the exchanged life. It is Christ, seeing through my eyes, walking in my shoes, touching with my hands, and speaking through my lips. It is "not I, but Christ!" Remember Galatians 2:20?

> *"I was crucified with Christ, nevertheless I live. Yet not I, but Christ liveth in me. And the life which I now live in the flesh, I live by the faith of the Son of God, who loved me and gave His life for me."*

You see, all of our programs and abilities and talents and gifts are absolutely NOTHING apart from the cutting edge of the Holy Spirit! Jesus said, in John 15:5, "...*without me, you can do nothing.*" We are nothing more than axe handles upon which swings the axe head of His life! The devil doesn't care what we do in ministry so long as we do it without the cutting edge of His power! If you sing or preach or witness to the lost or teach Sunday School without His power, it's akin to trying to chop down a tree with nothing but the axe handle!

Vance Havner said it best:

> *"Many of the Lord's workmen today have lost the axe head of power. They have lost the joy of salvation, they have not the upholding of God's Spirit. The lost axe head of the Spirit's unction has fallen into the waters of worldliness, the ponds of indifference, and the swamps of sluggishness. They have ability, training, sincerity, earnestness, but they are chopping with the handle. They stand before a demonized world powerless, and it must be said of them, as it was said of the disciples before the demonized boy, '...and they could not...'" (Mark 9:18). Oh! The pitiful tragedy of the lost axe head of the church today!"*

We need to be honest with ourselves and admit that we simply cannot do the work of God without the power of God! It is high time we found the lost axe head!

This may be surprising to some who are reading this, but it is not unusual to lose your cutting edge in the midst of doing church work. This young man was doing a good work. He was working for the Lord, but he lost his cutting edge. There may be some who are reading these words and you are doing some really good work for the Lord. You're doing the right things. You are busy and active in the building up of the church. You are working hard for the Lord, but you have noticed lately that there seems to be something missing. Have you lost your cutting edge? I can tell you that it is surprisingly easy in the midst of doing good things for God to lose your cutting edge. It is easy to get caught up in the work of the church and lose your cutting edge. Hear me when I say this: **Busyness does NOT equal spiritual!** Let me repeat that: **Busyness does not equal spiritual!** It is entirely possible to love the work of the Lord and not love the Lord of the work!

This young man was busy in the work of the Lord, but he still lost his cutting edge. And when you lose your cutting edge, you lose your effectiveness, your joy, your peace, and your passion. You lose your wonder.

Gypsy Smith, the great evangelist of the early 20th century, was an actual gypsy who got saved and was called to preach, and he was a fireball of a preacher. With a great sense of humor and a zest for life he used to say, "I was born in a field, so don't put me in a flowerpot." He loved to sing, but when someone told him he would sound better if he would learn to sing from his "diaphragm," he responded by saying, "I don't want to sing from my diaphragm, I want to sing from my heart!" When he was 87 years old, and still going strong, he was asked about the secret of his zeal and enthusiasm even into old age and his answer was, " I have never lost the wonder!"

When you lose your cutting edge, you lose your wonder. You become stale, jaded, cynical, cold, complacent, content, tired, weary, and hard hearted. The things that used to make you weep don't even phase you anymore. Sins that used to mortify you, now don't bother you much at all. Sound familiar?

Perhaps it's time you admitted to God that you have lost your cutting edge, and ask Him to lead you back to the place where you lost it, and get it back.

Genuine revival is all about Jesus. It's all about surrendering to Him, lock, stock, and barrel. If it's about anything else, it is not genuine revival. You may have miracles, but miracles will not be the focus. You may have healing, but healing will not be the focus. You may have great crowds, but great crowds will not replace Jesus as the focus. In true revival, Jesus Christ is center stage, and the Holy Spirit will always point to Him. So we need to get it down good, get it down big, and get it down right. Revival is about Jesus, surrendering to His Lordship, and rekindling our love for Him.

Dr. Adrian Rogers was in Romania spending time with Joseph Tson, the man who had been for many years the spiritual leader of that country. They began having a conversation about the difference between Christianity in Romania and America. Dr. Rogers recalls the conversation:

> *"Joseph, tell me what you think about American Christianity."*
>
> *Adrian, I'd rather not.*
>
> *No, I want you to.*
>
> *Well, Adrian, since you asked me, I will tell you. The key word in American Christianity is <u>commitment</u>.*
>
> *That's good, isn't it, Joseph?*
>
> *No, it is not. As a matter of fact, the word commitment did not come into great usage in the English language until about the 1960's. In Romania we do not even have a word to translate the English word commitment. If you were to use the word commitment in your message tonight, I would not have a proper word to translate it with. When a new word comes into usage, it generally pushes an old word out. I began to study and found the old word that commitment replaced. Adrian, the old word that is no longer in vogue in America is the word "surrender."*

> *Joseph, what is the difference between commitment and surrender?*
>
> *When you make a commitment, you are still in control, no matter how noble the thing you commit to. One can commit to pray, to study the Bible, to give his money, or to make automobile payments, or to lose weight. Whatever he chooses to do, he commits to. But surrender is different. If someone holds a gun and asks you to put your hands in the air as a token of surrender, you don't tell that person what you are committed to. You simply surrender and do as you are told. Americans love commitment because they are still in control. But the key word is surrender. We are to be the slaves of the Lord Jesus Christ."*

Joseph Tson couldn't be more right. Our problem in America is that we want to retain control. We want to control God instead of letting God control us. We devise our plan in committee meetings, set our course, write out our vision statement, and then hand it up to God and ask Him to sign on the dotted line. And when God doesn't bless our efforts, we start pointing fingers. We have replaced total surrender with conditional commitment to His will.

When we experience true revival, we will fall in love with Jesus all over again, and willingly, happily, gratefully surrender our will and our life to Him. We will learn to be patient in prayer, and refuse to move forward until we know that we have God's direction. Our hearts will burn with love for Him again, like the two men on the Emmaus road after they had walked with Jesus for a while. They said, *"Did not our hearts burn within us?"*

I heard about a lady named Ann Preston, who was nicknamed "Holy Ann" because of the holy life she lived. She could not read one word, but somehow, miraculously, she was able to read the Bible. One day somebody handed her a newspaper and asked her if she could read any words on the page. She went through the whole page and found one word she could read. It was the word, "Lord." The article was talking about some lord over in England. Holy Ann said, *"I can read that word, lord, but I don't think it is my Lord they are talking about because my heart doesn't burn when I read it."*

There was a time for many Christians when their heart "burned" for Jesus when they read his Word; when they thought about Him; when they talked about Him, or when they sang about Him. But not anymore. Their passion is gone. Their fire is gone. Their love for Jesus has waned. The desire is no longer there. Yes, they may still be active in church, but they are merely going through the motions; they've lost their first love. They desperately need revival.

There was a time in many churches when people walked the aisle and got saved. The people would get excited, clap their hands, and rejoice with tears running down their cheeks. Young people would surrender their lives to missions and to preach the gospel, and church was exciting, spontaneous, and unpredictable. It was glorious and joyful and fulfilling. But not anymore. Now, they just want to go home and take a nap. Now they don't care if anything happens in their church or not. All they're concerned about is getting out of church early enough to beat everybody else to the local restaurant.

Church, for many, has become predictable and boring. Those were two things the early church was never accused of! Michael Catt says that we have managed to do the one thing the enemies of Christ could never do to His church: we've made it boring. I think I've figured out the reason why most people don't attend church. It's because they've already been!

But when revival comes, things change. Church becomes exciting, unpredictable, and energized. Things begin to happen that man cannot explain, and man cannot produce. People begin getting saved, Christians begin to repent, relationships are reconciled, and Jesus becomes extraordinarily real as the Holy Spirit is no longer grieved or quenched. Suddenly, more than anything else, we want to see Jesus! Like those Greeks in the New Testament who said to Philip, *"Sirs, we want to see Jesus!"* Our whole life becomes preoccupied with Jesus Christ.

In Romans 1:1 Paul says he was *"separated unto the Gospel of Christ."* The Greek word there for "separated" is the word from which we get our word, "horizon." The horizon is that line of demarcation where the sky meets the earth. It is a clearly distinguishable line. When you look at the horizon, you can see clearly the line where the sky meets the earth. Paul knew exactly what his message was. His whole horizon was dominated by Jesus Christ! And ours will be too when we experience Revival!

Someone has said that the definition of a fanatic is "someone who won't change their mind and won't change the subject." That was the Apostle Paul!

> There was one message about which he talked!
>
> There was one desire that kept him motivated!
>
> There was one purpose for which he lived!
>
> There was one calling for which he strived!
>
> There was one goal in his life and it was to preach Jesus with his life and lips to his dying day!

He said, "For to me to live, is Christ, and to die, is gain!" He was saying,

> "I have no life but the life of Jesus in me!
>
> I have no vision, but Christ's vision for me!
>
> I have no purpose, but His purpose in me!
>
> I have no will, but His will for my life!"

It is safe to say that Paul was a fanatic about Jesus Christ. Or to put it another way, "He was on fire for Jesus." And shouldn't we all be?

Jesus was the summon bonum, the sum and circumference, the introduction, body and conclusion of Paul's message! Pastors, we must preach Jesus! And we must preach Him with enthusiasm! Vince Lombardi, the legendary coach of the Green Bay Packers once said, "If you're not fired with enthusiasm, you should be fired...with enthusiasm." And there is no person we should be more excited about than Jesus! And there is no message we should be more excited about preaching than "Jesus saves!" Preacher, whatever else you preach, make sure you preach Jesus! Stop chasing rabbits and trying to impress people with your oratorical skills, and just preach Jesus Christ crucified and raised again! We need to stop trying to be cute and clever in the pulpit and just preach the Gospel of Jesus Christ! If it was good enough for Paul when he preached to the erudite, metropolitan crowd at Corinth, it is good enough for us:

> *"And I, brethren, when I came to you, came not with excellency of speech or of wisdom, declaring unto to you the Gospel, for I determined not to know anything among you, save Jesus Christ, and him crucified. And I was with you in weakness, and in fear, and in much trembling. And my speech and my preaching was not with enticing words of man's wisdom, but in demonstration of the Spirit and of power. That your faith should not stand in the wisdom of men, but in the power of God."*

We who are charged with preaching the Gospel, are called to be prophets of God, not politicians. Enough of Critical Race Theory and Intersectionality, and Climate Change and Mother Earth Worship. Let's leave all that for the politicians. We are to preach Jesus, not our opinions about current events. *"And daily in the temple, and in every house, they did not cease teaching and preaching Jesus as the Christ"* (Acts 5:42). Eloquence and emotion are never substitutes for the Gospel. So let's just get back to preaching the only message that can keep people out of Hell—Jesus saves! That should be the throbbing heart of our message!

I'm afraid the world is asking for bread, and we are giving them stones. We should be like the cello player who all through the concert never moved her hand up or down the neck of the cello. Someone approached her afterwards and said, "I noticed all the other cellists were moving their hand up and down the neck, but yours never moved. How come?" She answered, "They were looking for it, but I found it."

My friend, if you are looking for God; if you're looking for peace; if you're looking for purpose in life, when you find Jesus, your search is over. It may sound terribly oversimplified, but Andre Crouch was right years ago when he sang, "Jesus is the answer, for the world today. Above Him there's no other, Jesus is the way!" That may sound outdated and old fashioned, but so is the Sun, so is air, and so is water. But try living without any one of those. It is true. Jesus is the answer. He really is! He said, "W*hen you've seen me, you've seen the Father.*"

No wonder Luther Bridges would write, "*Jesus, Jesus, Jesus, sweetest name I know. Fills my every longing, keeps me singing as I go.*"

Dear friend, those of us who have been saved by Jesus, need to live for Jesus, love Jesus, and preach Jesus! Are you saved? Have you been redeemed? Has He washed away your sins in His own precious blood? Have you been rescued by Him, "as a brand plucked from the fire," as John Wesley once said? Is He the lover of your soul? Then let us preach the message of Jesus with our life and with our lips to a lost and dying world!

It thrills me to hear Gardner C. Taylor, that great Black preacher, exalting the magnificence of Jesus Christ in his sermon, "Our Great Savior." Hear his words and let God stir your heart to fall in love with Jesus once again!

> "*I LOVE TO TALK ABOUT HIM! I do! I love to say His name! It's a simple name. A beautiful name. The name above every name. The name of Jesus. Say it out loud. Again. One more time! Now, did you hear the demons scurrying and running for cover? They can't stand that name!*
>
> *In Philippians 2:5-7, Paul talks about the humility of our Lord. He exchanged the adulation of Heavenly creatures for the curses of men. And this is the gospel in miniature. This is salvation history in two or three sentences. This is what it is all about. This is the living heart; the throbbing core of the gospel. Everything else is tributary and derivative. But this is the throbbing center of what our faith is all about. That he gave up his hometown in glory, and became a stranger in the earth. Jesus! In our interest, left his natural state*

of preeminence and came here to this low land of sorrow to be mocked and ridiculed. He took upon himself the form of a servant, for our interest. For our salvation. He became one of us. Death eligible! Pain capable! For you. And for me. He humbled himself.

Isaac Watts wrote:

"Was it for crimes that I had done,

He groaned upon the tree;

Amazing pity, grace unknown, and love beyond degree.

Well might the sun in darkness hide,

And shut his glories in,

When Christ, the mighty Maker died,

For man, the creature's sin."

And because He did, we who are sinners deserving of Death and Hell, have hope.

He has been my friend…for so long.

He has led my feet; guided me; protected me; I LOVE TO TALK ABOUT HIM!

He was born contrary to the laws of birth, and died triumphant over the laws of death.

He was born in poverty, but wise men brought their riches and laid them at his feet.

He was cradled in another's crib, sailed on another's boat, rode on another's animal.

He had his last supper in another's upper room, was laid to rest in another's tomb, but to Him belong the unsearchable riches of glory!

The earth is His and the fullness thereof.

And the cattle on a thousand hills are all His.

He never wrote but once, and that in the disappearing sands of the Temple, but all the libraries of the world cannot contain the books that have been written about Him.

We know of one instance only in which He sang a hymn, but the most creative geniuses of melody have brought their purest gifts and laid them reverently at His feet.

As a baby, He frightened a King.

As a child, He perplexed the elders and doctors.

As a man, he made the sea be still, and made the boisterous waves lie down upon the bosom of his gentle command.

Sin could not seduce Him.

Satan could not resist Him.

Sinners could not withstand Him.

Death could not destroy Him.

Demons could not bind Him.

And the grave could not hold Him.

I LOVE TO TALK ABOUT MY SAVIOR!

I LOVE TO HONOR HIM!

He is a friend in loneliness.

He is strength in weakness.

He is health in sickness.

He is the widow's pension.

He is the prisoner's pardon.

He is the exile's recall to citizenship.

He is the orphan's adoption.

I LOVE! I LOVE! I LOVE TO TALK ABOUT HIM!

JESUS! An answer in one word!

JESUS! An oratorical wonder in two syllables!

JESUS! JESUS! JESUS! JESUS! JESUS! MY LORD! I KNOW HIS NAME!"

Does reading that just now warm your heart and thrill your soul? I am literally trembling from just typing out those powerful words. My heart is on fire for Jesus even now! Oh, how we need to vibrate once again with a holy excitement that we get to tell people the old, old story of Jesus and His love! Those who know me know that I am a passionate, emotional person. I get excited about Jesus and His cross. And I am not ashamed of it! I don't ever want to get over it!

Isn't it about time we got noticeably excited and enthused about what God has done for us in Jesus Christ? Haven't we given "normal" Christianity long enough to get the job done? Hasn't the "usual" had long enough? Haven't we been "ordinary" long enough and yet we still haven't seen revival in our great land? What I believe we need today is an **extra**ordinary, **un**usual, **super**natural move of the Holy Spirit in revival! That will get the job done! What does it matter if our message is eloquent, our teaching sound, and our presentation proper, if there is no fire, no passion and no breath of God on it? Some years ago I heard a preacher say, in reference modern day Christianity, that "we have been "subnormal" for so long that when somebody comes along who is "normal," we think he is "abnormal."

It has been said that one person with passion is worth more than 10,000 with interest alone! Don't be shy to talk about your Savior! Don't be namby-pamby about the greatest message the world has ever heard! Jim Elliot, the martyred missionary to the Auca Indians, once said, "We need to repent of preaching a dynamite gospel and living firecracker lives!"

I want to remind you that we who call ourselves Christians are followers of the One who said, *"For zeal for Thy house hath consumed me."* (Ps. 69:9) And *"I will make my ministers a flame of fire."* (Ps. 104:40)

Listen, my friend! Our Lord Jesus was a passionate, exciting person! He was completely consumed with a passion to complete God's purpose for His life, and He followed that passion to the Cross to die for our sins that we might be saved.

And it was THIS Jesus, of whom John said, "He will baptize you with fire!" The symbol of Pentecost was not a noodle, but a flame of fire! After they were filled with the Spirit, discouraged, doubting, and despairing disciples had every fear and barrier melted away as they were consumed with a flaming passion for Christ!

The early disciples tarried in Jerusalem until they were endued with the power of the Holy Spirit and they went out in that power with the name of Jesus on their lips and turned the world upside down for Jesus!

That is the power of the message of Jesus Christ! That is what caused one of the early church Fathers to proclaim, "If the whole world were my parish; and the heavens my pulpit, then Jesus alone would be my message!"

The writer, James Allen Francis, wrote an immortal piece of prose that expounds upon the uniqueness of Jesus. It is called "One Solitary Life":

> *Here is a man who was born in an obscure village, the child of a peasant woman. He grew up in another obscure village, where He worked in a carpenter shop until He was thirty, and then for three years He was an itinerant preacher. He never wrote a book. He never held an office. He never owned a home. He never had a family. He never went to college. He never put his foot inside a big city. He never traveled two hundred miles from the place where He was born. He never did one of the things that usually accompany greatness. He had no credentials but Himself. He had nothing to do with this world except the naked power of His divine manhood. While still a young man, the tide of public opinion turned against Him. His friends ran away. One of them denied Him. He was turned over to His enemies. He went through the mockery of a trial. He was nailed to a cross between two thieves. His executioners gambled for the only piece of property He had on earth while*

He was dying—and that was His coat. When He was dead He was taken down and laid in a borrowed grave through the pity of a friend. Nineteen wide centuries have come and gone and today He is the centerpiece of the human race and the leader of the column of progress. I am far within the mark when I say that all the armies that have ever marched, and all the navies that were ever built, and all the parliaments that ever sat, all the kings that ever reigned, put together have not affected the life of man upon this earth as powerfully as has that ONE SOLITARY LIFE.

And this is magnificently true! Charles Lamb, the poet, said, *"If Shakespeare were to come into this room, we would all rise to our feet, but if Jesus Christ were to enter, we would all fall upon our knees!"*

Colossians 1:15 tells us that Jesus is *"the firstborn over all creation and by Him all things were created in heaven and in earth!"*

That means that it was Jesus who:

"Came from nowhere, because there was nowhere to come from;

Stood on nothing, because there was nothing to stand on;

Spoke to nobody, because there was nobody to speak to;

And called something out of nothing, and something came forth and hung out there in nothing, and it stayed there because Jesus said it, and it was so!"

It was Jesus who put:

The Bark in the dog

The Meow in the cat

The Oink in the pig

The Laugh in the hyena

The Moo in the cow, and

The Quack in the duck.

It was Jesus who wrote **every tune** that a mockingbird sings!

It was Jesus who put:

The Splendor in the roses

The fragrance in the tulips

The Honey in the honeysuckle, and

T**he wonder** in them all!

Shadrack Meshack Lockridge, better known as S.M. Lockridge, gave us a sermonic treat some years ago in a sermon called, "That's My King!": He said,

*I wonder **if you know Him**.*

*Don't try to mislead me. **Do you know my King?***

The Bible says He's the King of the Jews.

He's the King of Righteousness.

He's the King of the Ages.

He's the King of Heaven.

He's the King of Glory.

He's the King of Kings and the Lord of Lords.

Now that's My King.

Well, No means of measure can define his limitless love.

No far-seeing telescope can bring into visibility the coastline of his shoreless supply.

No barrier can hinder him from pouring out his blessings.

No far seeing telescope can bring into visibility the coastline of His shoreless supply.

He is enduringly strong/ He is entirely sincere/ He is eternally steadfast/ He is immortally graceful/ He is imperially powerful/ and He is impartially merciful.

That's my King.

He's the greatest phenomenon that has ever crossed the horizon of this world.

He's God's Son

He's the sinner's Savior

He's the centerpiece of civilization.

He stands in the solitude of Himself.

He is august and He's unique.

He's unparalleled.

He's unprecedented.

He's the loftiest idea in literature.

He's the highest personality in philosophy

He's the supreme problem in Higher Criticism.

He's the fundamental doctrine of true theology.

He's the core, the necessity for spiritual religion.

He's the miracle of the age!

Do you know Him?

He's the summon bonum of everything righteous.

He's the sum and circumference of all that is pure.

He's the superlative of everything good that you choose to call Him.

He's the only one qualified to be an all-sufficient Savior.

I wonder, do you know Him?

He supplies strength for the weak.

He's available for the tempted and tried.

He sympathizes and He saved.

He guards and He guides.

He heals the sick.

He cleansed the lepers.

He forgives sinners.

He discharges debtors.

He delivers the captives.

He defends the feeble.

He blesses the young.

He serves the unfortunate.

He regards the aged.

He rewards the diligent.

And He purifies the meek.

Do you know Him? Do you know my King?

Well....

He's the key to knowledge.

He's the wellspring of wisdom.

He's the doorway of deliverance.

He's the Pathway of peace.

He's the Roadway of Righteousness.

He's the Highway of Holiness.

He's the Gateway of Glory.

Do you know Him?

Oh, His office is manifold.

His promise is sure.

His light is matchless.

His goodness is limitless.

His mercy is everlasting.

His love never changes.

His Word is enough.

His grace is sufficient.

His reign is righteousness.

His yoke is easy.

And His burden is light.

I wonder, do you Know Him?

Oh, I wish I could describe Him to you tonight!

But He is indescribable.

He is Incomprehensible!

He is Invincible!

He is Irresistible!

Well, I've come to tell you,

The heaven of heavens cannot contain Him,

Let alone a man explain Him.

You can't get him out of your mind/ off your hand/ and away from your heart!

You can't outlive him, and you can't live without him

The Pharisees couldn't stand Him, but they found out they couldn't stop him!

Pilate couldn't find any fault with Him.

The witnesses couldn't confuse him.

Herod couldn't kill him.

Sin couldn't conquer him.

The devil couldn't defeat him.

Death couldn't handle him, and

The grave couldn't hold him.

That's my King!

He always has been, and he always will be.

He had no predecessor

And He will have no successor

There was nobody before Him,

And there'll be nobody after Him,

You can't impeach Him and He's not going to resign.

That's my King! Do you know Him?

He's the Master of the Mighty

He's the Captain of the Conquerors

He's the Head of the Heroes

He's the Leader of the Legislators

He's the Overseer of the Overcomers

He's the Governor of Governors

He's the Prince of Princes

He's the King of Kings

And He's the Lord of Lords!

S. M. Lockridge is right! Jesus Christ is the King of Kings and Lord of Lords. And in Heaven today He is adored as Heaven's darling prince. Atheists and Agnostics may dismiss Him today, skeptics may laugh and ridicule him, and critics may scoff at Him, but you can be certain that there is coming a day when *"...at the name of Jesus, every knee shall bow, of things in heaven, and things on earth, and things under the earth, and every tongue shall confess that Jesus Christ is Lord, to the glory of God the Father!" (Phil. 2: 10-11)*

There are some things that can be said about Jesus that cannot be said about any other person. Consider this:

> Jesus was seen in the fiery furnace before he was ever born!
>
> Jesus was alive before he was ever born!
>
> Jesus is older than his mother!
>
> Jesus is as old as His Father!
>
> Jesus was the glory that filled the tabernacle!
>
> Jesus was the cloud by day and ball of fire by night.
>
> Jesus was the Rock in the wilderness!
>
> Jesus was Ezekiel's wheel in the middle of the wheel!
>
> Jesus was the fire in the bush that burned!
>
> Jesus was the 4th man in the fire!
>
> Jesus is the Jewel in the city of God!

The Bible says the winds are His messengers, the clouds are His chariots, the fire is His servant and the waters flee at His command!

His ways are right, His Word is eternal, His will is unchanging, and His mind is on me!

He's my Redeemer; my Savior; my guide; and my peace!

He's my Joy, my comfort, my Lord and He rules my life!

When I fall, He lifts me up!

When I fail, He forgives!

When I am weak, He is strong!

When I am lost, He is the Way!

When I am afraid, He is my courage!

When I stumble, He steadies me!

When I am hurt, He heals me!

When I am broken, He mends me!

When I am blind, he leads me!

When I am hungry, He feeds me!

When I face trials, He is with me!

When I face persecution, He shields me!

When I face problems, He comforts me!

When I face loss, He provides for me!

When I face death, He carries me home!

Jesus is everything to everybody. It matters not who you are or what your need may be, I say to you on the authority of the Word of God and with 100% certainty that Jesus is the answer for you!

He is the Alpha and Omega, the First and the Last, the Beginning and the End. Alpha is the first letter of the Greek alphabet. Omega is the last letter of the Greek alphabet. That's like saying, Jesus is the A to the Z of our alphabet.

To the Artist, He's the One Altogether Lovely.

To the Astronomer, He's the Bright and Morning Star.

To the Architect, He's the Chief Cornerstone.

To the Baker, He's the Bread of Life.

To the Biologist, He's the Author of Life.

To the Builder, He's the Sure Foundation.

To the Carpenter, He's the Door.

To the Doctor, He's the Great Physician.

To the Educator, He's the Master Teacher.

To the Farmer, He's Sower and Lord of the Harvest.

To the Geologist, He's the Rock of Ages.

To the Horticulturist, He's the True Vine, the Lily of the Valley, and the Rose of Sharon.

To the Israelite, He's the Messiah of God.

To the Jeweler, He's the Pearl of Great Price.

To the Juror, He's the Faithful and True Witness.

To the King, He's the King of Kings.

To the Lonely, He's the Friend who sticks closer than a brother.

To the Mortician, He's the Resurrection and the Life.

To the Monarch, He's the Potentate of Potentates.

To the Nurse, He's the Balm of Gilead.

To the Newspaper Boy, He's the Good News of Great Joy.

To the Oceanographer, He's the Water of Life.

To the Philosopher, He's the Wisdom of God.

To the Poor, He's the Unspeakable Gift.

To the Preacher, He's the Amen.

To the Quitter, He's the Author and Finisher of our Faith.

To the Royal Family, He's the Prince of Peace.

To the Shepherd, He's the Lamb of God that takes away the sins of the world.

To the Sheep, He's the Good Shepherd, the Great Shepherd, and the Shepherd and Bishop of our souls.

To the Sinner, He's our Redeemer, our Savior, and our Soon Coming King.

To the Time Keeper, He's the One who Was, Who is, and Who is to Come.

To the Undertaker, He's the One who was dead and is alive again and has the keys to death and Hell at His side.

To the Victim, He's the Good Samaritan.

To the Weary, He's the Burden Bearer.

To the X-Ray Technician, He's the Image of the Invisible God.

To the Young, He's the Ancient of Days.

To the Zoologist, He's the Lion of the Tribe of Judah.

No matter who you are. No matter where you live. No matter what you've done. No matter what you need. No matter how many problems you have or how confused you are. Jesus is all you need!

So what should we do with Him? We should bow our knees before Him and crown Him Lord and Savior of our lives!

When Victoria was just a teenager, she was crowned Queen of England. In preparation for her coronation, it was arranged that the climax would be the singing of Handel's Hallelujah chorus, from Messiah. The young queen was raised in modest seclusion, and had to be taught the protocol of the Court. So she was informed that though everyone else should rise during the singing of that great oratorio, she must not rise. It would not be proper for royalty. Her position was too dignified.

Everything went as planned until the concluding moments of the presentation. As the choir began to sing, "And He shall reign forever and ever," the young queen began to tremble with deep emotion. And when the singers reached those all-glorious words: "King of Kings and Lord of Lords, King of Kings, and Lord of Lords," she could no longer remain seated. Against all the instructions she had been given, she rose, lifted her eyes heavenward, and then bowed her head and wept.

And shouldn't we all? Shouldn't we all? He is the King of Kings. He is the Lord of Lords. Let us, therefore, love him, adore him, ever speak of him, and serve him till the day we die. And when we see him face to face, we can fall on our faces before him and sing,

> All hail the power of Jesus' name, let angels prostrate fall.
> Bring forth the royal diadem and crown him Lord of all!

This is what genuine revival does for us. It brings us to Jesus. We see Him for who He really is, and we fall in love with Him all over again as we surrender to His claim to be Lord of our lives. We must! We must! We must have revival!

9

CHARACTERISTIC # 6 PRAYER

A NEW PASSION AND URGENCY IN PRAYER

"The only power that God yields to is that of prayer. We will write about prayer power, but not fight while in prayer. A title, undeniably true of the church today, would be 'We wrestle not!' We will display our gifts, natural or spiritual; we will air our views, political or spiritual; we will preach a sermon or write a book to correct a brother in doctrine. But who will storm Hell's stronghold? Who will say the devil nay? Who will deny himself good food or good company or good rest that Hell may gaze upon him wrestling, embarrassing demons, liberating captives, depopulating Hell, and leaving, in answer to his travail, a stream of blood-washed souls?"
--Leonard Ravenhill in "Why Revival Tarries."

Revival must not only be *preceded* by prayer, revival must also be *sustained* by prayer. Prayer opens the floodgates of revival to be sure, but when true revival comes, God's people will find themselves drawn to prayer. Deep, pleading, intercessory prayer.

It was Matthew Henry who observed, *"When God intends a blessing for His people, He sets them a praying."* The secret to the outpouring of the Spirit of God in revival throughout history has been prayer. There have been many revivals that took place without great preaching, singing, or organization, but there has never been a mighty move of God in revival without mighty praying. It cannot be disputed that prayer has been the ignition to every revival fire in history, and the key that unlocks the door of ministry for every preacher used by God in the past.

The First Great Awakening came about because of a young minister in Northampton, Massachusetts named Jonathan Edwards, who was a brilliant mind and a great theologian (He enrolled in Yale at the age of 12), though not a dynamic speaker. He spoke in a monotone voice and his eyes were so bad that he basically had to bend down to read his scripted sermons word for word with coke-bottle glasses.

But oh, the power that fell when he would preach! It is said that when he would preach his famous sermon, "Sinners in the Hands of an Angry God," men and women would swoon and hold onto the posts in the church to keep from feeling like they were falling into Hell. At times there would be such a commotion among the congregation that Edwards could not be heard, and he would stop and request that they refrain from weeping and crying out in order to hear the rest of his sermon! If it was not his oratory, then what was the secret to his power? He prayed for hours upon hours until his heart was aflame with the fire of the Spirit. Jonathan Edwards prayed and then preached, and the First Great Awakening came, bringing over 50,000 people to faith in Christ.

In 1806, there were five college students who had begun to pray twice a week for a mighty move of God to occur. At least one of these men had been touched by the Second Great Awakening under George Whitfield and the Wesley brothers, John and Charles. One hot and sultry Saturday afternoon, these five students at Williams College in Williamstown, Massachusetts, were on their way to their prayer meeting off campus (prayer was basically forbidden on campus), when a severe thunderstorm caught them by surprise. They huddled together under a haystack for shelter and prayed for

God to meet with them. Here is what one historical account said happened next:

> *"Finally, after singing a hymn, Mills looked at the others, and over the roar of the drenching rain, and with flashes of lightning reflecting in his eyes, cried out, 'We can do this, if we will!' Something broke loose in that moment within the hearts of all five. All five pointed back to that moment as the one that changed them forever. And all five later surrendered themselves to Missions and carried the gospel around the world. That moment in 1806 under the haystack was the spark for the greatest missionary movement the world has ever seen. The sheer numbers of missionary agencies birthed and missionaries called overseas, including Adoniram and Anne Judson as well as Luther Rice, are absolutely staggering."*

The revival that ensued touched all of New England and came to be known as The Haystack Revival. It is said that the modern missions movement can be traced directly to the Haystack Prayer Meeting.

The Great Revival of 1857-58 began with a small prayer meeting led by a layman named Jeremiah Lamphere. He was a member of the Dutch Reformed Church on Fulton Street in New York City. His church was suffering. People were moving out to the suburbs, and it was a downtown church. The area around the church was becoming extremely poverty stricken and blighted. And so the church appointed Jeremiah Lamphere to be a lay missionary who would minister to the people around that church. As Lamphere made his visits, he could not help but notice the looks of apprehension and anxiety on the faces of the businessmen he met on the streets of New York City. They knew that this nation was standing on the verge of economic disaster. A bubble of prosperity that had been building for years was about to burst, and businessmen were aware of that.

Jeremiah Lamphere had the idea that it would be a good thing to call these men to prayer, so he widely distributed and circulated publicity, saying that on the second Wednesday in the month of

September on the 3rd floor assembly room of the Dutch Reformed church on Fulton Street, at 12:00 noon, a prayer meeting would be held for businessmen.

At 12:00 noon, Lamphere was there, alone. He prayed alone for about 15 minutes. I imagine he had butterflies in his stomach. 20 minutes passed...25 minutes.... Butterflies had turned to buzzards because nobody came. At 12:30 he heard a footfall on the stair outside the door, and then another, and another, and another until five other men had joined him to launch the Fulton Street Prayer Meetings. They prayed together and they were so encouraged by the prayers that they agreed to meet the next Wednesday for prayer again. This time, 20 businessmen came. They agreed to meet again the next Wednesday and this time, 40 businessmen came. The next Wednesday, 100 were there, many of them lost, and they agreed to have these prayer meetings every single day. Within 5 weeks, every single room in the North Dutch Reformed Church on Fulton Street was crowded out with praying men and the there were some standing on the outside who simply couldn't get in.

Since there was such a hunger to pray, a second church was opened for prayer, the John Street Methodist Church, not far away. The first day it was opened, it was so packed with praying men that there were scores on the outside that just couldn't find anyplace inside the building. They then opened Burton's Theatre in downtown New York City, the largest theatre in the city. Along with Fulton Street and John Street, the theatre was opened for noonday prayer meetings and one newspaper reported that the building "was stuffed from pit to dome;" that is, from the orchestra pit to the 3rd floor balcony, and there were hundreds milling around on the outside who simply couldn't get in. Within six months, there were 150 prayer meetings like this going on in New York City alone and 50,000 New Yorkers were pausing daily to pray. It goes without saying that you cannot puncture heaven with that kind of praying without the blessings of revival beginning to fall! And fall they did! People were praying everywhere! No sooner was a new place of prayer announced that hundreds of people flocked to it. New York

City found herself in the midst of the greatest revival she had ever known in her colorful history.

It was nothing on Sunday mornings to see a hundred people come forward for salvation in some of those churches, openly confessing Jesus as their Savior. Within a few short weeks, 90,000 people had been converted to Christ in the great Metropolis of New York City! Revival flowed out from the city into other regions of the country, down the Eastern Seaboard and around the nation.

The press caught hold of what God was doing in New York City. Some newspapers ran revival extras just to tell the latest stories of the work of God in some community or some city. At no time in history has the work of our Lord Jesus been so widely publicized by the media as it was in 1858. But somebody early on referred to it as the "Prayer Revival" and that was appropriate because every major city and most small towns in this country had organized daily prayer meetings. One man rode a train from Omaha, Nebraska to New York City, which is about 1500 miles, and this was in the day before there was anything known as "an express," so the train stopped at every little village and town along the way. And he said that in every village or town the train stopped, there was a prayer meeting going on as the Spirit of God swept across the country. It became known as "the 1500 mile Prayer Meeting."

Efforts were made in this revival to reach people of particular professions. For example, 1500 firemen in Philadelphia were converted to Jesus, and there were 35 firehouses where prayer meetings were going on every day.

One of the thrilling chapters of the revival of 1858 had to do with the U.S. Navy. The battleship *North Carolina* was what we would call a training ship, and it was berthed in New York Harbor. One day four sailors came to the captain and asked him if they could hold a prayer meeting down inside the hull, the lower part of the ship. Now that was something new—a prayer meeting on a battleship! But they were granted permission and as they prayed, they were so caught up in prayer that they began to praise the Lord out loud and they began to sing to the Lord. The other sailors heard them singing and praising, and almost to a man they ran to ridicule and mock these four sailors. However, when they got within a few feet of these praying men, they hit a "fire zone" of the Holy Spirit where they were deeply convicted of their sins; many were converted on the spot. Within a matter of hours, 46 men had been converted on the *USS North Carolina*. These men would leave this training ship and serve on other ships and revival would break out on them as well. It seemed that there was a zone of heavenly influence around the eastern coastline of this country. Time after time, ships would dock that had never heard of revival going on in this country, but they would dock with a story something like this: "A few miles out our ship was gripped by conviction for sin and passengers were converted and the captain was converted and the crew was converted." As many as 30 captains of ships came into ports on the eastern seaboard declaring that they had been converted when they hit this invisible zone of heavenly influence just a few miles out from the coastline of this country.

At the peak of this revival, some 50,000 people per month were being converted all across the country. For two whole years, some 10,000 people a week joined the church. Incredible, incredible stories of conversion came from this mighty revival that began with one man and a prayer meeting!

It is impossible to overemphasize the power of prayer as it relates to revival. Every revival had prayer as a major factor. If by some miracle of God we could see how many tragedies could have been averted, how many lives could have been spared, how many battles would not have been lost, how many souls could have been kept out of the fires of Hell, how many marriages would not have broken up, and how many churches would not have had to close its doors, if only we would have prayed, then we would all fall on our faces today and set ourselves wholly to the ministry of prayer!

It's time for the church of the Lord Jesus Christ to stop "saying prayers" and learn how to pray. I'm afraid so much of our praying is like the young lawyer I heard about who had just opened up a brand new office. He was seated behind his shiny new desk eagerly awaiting his first client. He heard footsteps in the hall and a hand on the doorknob. Wanting to look important, he pretended to be busy and picking up the telephone carried on a fake conversation. "Yes, yes, I'll have my secretary tend to that as soon as I can get to it. I have a very busy schedule. Call back tomorrow and we'll get it taken care of." Motioning toward the door, he said to the man, "Come in, come in." So the man stepped inside the room and stood there listening to one end of this high-powered conversation. Finally, the lawyer hung up the phone and said, "How can I help you? The man said, "Well, I'm from the phone company and I've come to hook up your telephone."

Is it possible that all too often we are praying to seen by men, or praying out of routine, or praying because someone said we should, but our heart's not in it, and there is no one on the other end of the line? Maybe the reason the church is not winning the lost to Christ, setting the captives free, driving out the demons, and storming the gates of Hell is because prayer has become the most neglected ministry of the church! If our churches were as lax concerning our finances as we are concerning prayer, most of them would be bankrupt in 90 days! You can ask any church to list its ministries, and not one in twenty-five would have any kind of organized, consistent prayer ministry. Prayer is what provides warmth in a church; you cannot hatch eggs in a refrigerator!

Paul said, "Praying always." (Ephesians 6:18)

Jesus said, "Men ought always to pray, and not faint." (Luke 18:1)

It is prayer that binds the devil and his bands of demons!

It is prayer that drives the enemy out of God's territory!

It is prayer that sets the captives free!

It is prayer that bombards the spiritual strongholds of the devil until they crumble in defeat!

It is prayer that unleashes the power of heaven!

It is prayer that releases the angelic hosts to aid the saints of God!

It is prayer that enables us to become "more than conquerors" over all the power of the enemy!

It is prayer that Satan fears most from a child of God!

The mightiest of demons has to flee when the weakest of saints bends his knee!

Charles Spurgeon, the Prince of Preachers, once said, *"I have no confidence at all in the polished speech or brilliant literary effort to bring about a revival, but I have all the confidence in the world in the poor saint who would weep her eyes out because people are living in sin."*

Prayer is vital to revival. You cannot have revival without heartfelt prayer. Prayer is to revival what labor is to childbirth. The joyous rapture of childbirth and holding that newborn baby in her arms, comes only after hours of labor pains and travail prior to the baby's birth. Likewise, there will never be genuine revival apart from our willingness to agonize through the labor pains of prevailing, pleading prayer.

I came across a poem last year by Mary Wharburton Booth entitled *"A Passionate Passion."* I liked it so much I committed it to memory. Here is the poem:

> A Passionate Passion
>
> Oh! For a heart that is burdened!
> Infused with a passion to pray;
> Oh! For a stirring within me;
> Oh! For His power every day.
> Oh! For a heart like my Savior,
> Who, being in an agony, prayed.
> Such caring for others, Lord, give me;
> On my heart let burdens be laid.
> My Father, I long for this passion,
> To pour myself out for the lost;

> To lay down my life to save others;
> To pray, whatever the cost.
> Lord, teach me, Oh teach me this secret
> I'm hungry this lesson to learn,
> This passionate passion for others,
> For this, blessed Jesus, I yearn.
> Father, this lesson I long for from Thee
> Oh, let Thy Spirit reveal this to me."

For the last several years God has been teaching me this passion in prayer. More specifically, how to *plead* in prayer for others. In my 45 years of ministry I have heard many sermons on prayer, read many books on prayer, and preached on various aspects of prayer, just like most ministers do. But one area of prayer I have heard virtually nothing about is *pleading* in prayer. Spurgeon, however, spoke of it often:

> *"It is the habit of faith, when she is praying to use pleas. Mere prayer-sayers who do not pray at all, forget to argue with God; but those who would prevail bring forth their reasons and their strong arguments and they debate the question with the Lord. Faith's art of wrestling is to plead with God, and say with a holy boldness, 'Let it be thus and thus, for these reasons.' Oh, brethren! Let us learn this: to plead the precepts, the promises, and whatever else may serve our turn; but let us always have something to plead. Do not reckon you have prayed unless you have pleaded, for pleading is the very marrow of prayer. He who pleads well knows the secret of prevailing with God, especially if he pleads the blood of Jesus, for that unlocks the treasury of heaven. Many keys fit many locks, but the master key is the blood and the name of Him that died and rose again, and ever lives in heaven to save unto the uttermost."*

My friend, we need to realize that there is much more to prayer than just asking for this or for that. God is not some benevolent bellhop running up and down the corridors of Heaven to find things to bring down to us to satisfy our every whim and want. God is not some kind of sanctified Santa Claus or glorified grocery store clerk running up and down the aisles of Heaven's grocery store collecting up the things we have given Him on our shopping list of wants. Prayer, real prayer, is much more than that. Prayer is powerful! Billy Sunday used to say that if you are a stranger to prayer you are a stranger to the most powerful force in the universe! And "pleading prayer," is the crème de la-crème of prayer.

In January of 2016, my pastor and I flew to Richmond, VA to the International Mission Board's Learning Center, where every Southern Baptist international missionary goes for training before they leave for the mission field. We went for something called Missions College, which is a week of intensive training in overseas missions. Our purpose was to get the training we needed to launch a partnership with the mission work in Lima, Peru.

Each evening there would be worship led by a worship team and a message from a preacher. One night, Dr. Gordon Fort was speaking on the subject of prayer, and in the course of his message he referred to a Greek word, which he said was the most powerful word on prayer in the New Testament. Even though I spent two years in college studying New Testament Greek, I had never heard this word before. But when Dr. Fort defined the word, it got my attention. The word was proseuchomai, and he defined it as "pleading the case" or "prosecuting the case." Then, Dr. Fort asked a troubling question. "Whose case are you pleading before the Throne of God today?" I immediately felt a stab of conviction, because I could not answer the question! Surprised at this word I was unfamiliar with, and now under conviction because I was not pleading anyone's case before God, I couldn't wait to get back home to my books to dig into the Word and find what this word meant.

Little did I know that this one word, "proseuchomai," would turn my prayer life upside down, (or should I say, "right side up") forever! It didn't take me long to realize that I knew absolutely nothing about this kind of praying. In the next few pages I would like to share with you <u>the greatest lesson on prayer God has ever taught me</u> and I will be forever grateful to Dr. Gordon Fort for opening my eyes to this principle and for some of the material in this section.

In James 5:16-18 there are actually two Greek words every believer needs to know. First, let's look at the passage:

> *"Confess your trespasses to one another, and* **pray** *for one another, that you may be healed. The <u>effective, fervent</u>* **prayer** *of a righteous man avails much. Elijah was a man with a nature like ours, and he* **prayed** *earnestly that it would not rain, and it did not rain on the land for three years and six months. And he* **prayed** *again, and the heaven gave rain, and the earth produced its fruit."*

In this text, the two words "effective" and "fervent" are translated from one Greek word, *"energeo."* And the word "energeo" means what it sounds like it might mean: "energetic; powerful; passionate." It is used 21 times in the New Testament and literally describes something that happens that cannot be contained. "Energeo" refers to something that when present, has the power to wield incredible influence.

It can be used negatively of the flesh, and we all know that when the flesh is in control of our life, when the big "I" is on the throne, when we are walking in the flesh, it can have an incredibly negative influence in our life. And we know how it can quickly get out of control.

But it can also be used positively of the Spirit. When the Spirit is in control of our life; when Jesus is on the throne; when we are walking in the Spirit, there is also an incredible influence for God that takes place in your life, and supernatural things can happen! It's the "effective, fervent" prayer that avails much. It's the "effective, fervent" prayer that makes powerful things happen!

This word describes a type of praying that is just the opposite of how most of us pray. Let's just admit it: Most of our normal praying is very nonchalant, very casual, very routine; usually it's "on the fly" and sometimes, well, I must say, even boring. Now, maybe your prayer life is dynamic and exemplary, but mine wasn't.

Before I learned this word, I would never have used words like effective, energetic, passionate, or powerful to describe my prayer life. And the sad thing about it is I had been a pastor for almost 40 years! Yet my prayer life was desperately lacking something, and I knew it.

"Energeo" describes a type of praying that takes hold of God and won't let go. And when we pray with that kind of power and tenacity, then incredible, supernatural spiritual things can happen. And that's what James 5:16-17 is saying. Elijah was a normal man like us. He was not perfect, nor was he above sin. He was, according to James 5:17, "a man with a nature like ours." Yet when he prayed, it didn't rain for 3 ½ years! Then he prayed again, and it rained. Now that is praying with power!

The second word in this passage is the word "proseuchomai." And I have come to believe that this is the most powerful prayer word in the Bible. The words "pray" and "prayer" are used four times in this passage, and every time it is the word "proseuchomai." In fact, this is the most predominant word for prayer in the whole New Testament. In various forms, it is used 127 times. It is a compound word from the preposition "pros" and "euche," which is the root word for prayer. "Euche" means *"a strong wish, a strong desire, or prayer."*

"Pros" means *"toward"* and denotes a sense of closeness; or *"close, personal contact."* It is used in John 1:1 to portray the intimate, up close, personal relationship that exists between the members of the Godhead: God the Father, God the Son, and God the Holy Spirit." John 1:1 states: *"In the beginning was the Word, and the Word was **with** God, and the Word was God."*

The word "with" is taken from this Greek word *"pros"* and describes the intratrinitarian harmony that has existed between the Father, Son, and Holy Spirit for all eternity. Within the Trinity, there is a close, intimate personal fellowship, which has never, ever been broken. In fact, one expositor translates that verse this way, *"In the beginning was the Word and the Word was **face to face** with God."* What a beautiful way to portray the close, personal fellowship between Father, Son and Holy Spirit!

The word "pros" is also used in the spiritual warfare section of Ephesians 6. Here, it depicts the believer's close contact with unseen demonic spirits in spiritual warfare. The word translated "against" is the word "pros" and is used six times to describe our relationship with our opponent in spiritual warfare. It carries the meaning of "personal, up close contact," in this case with regard to demonic spirits. Paul is saying that our warfare with the enemy of our soul is not akin to lobbing mortars from a mile away, but rather it is "hand to hand" combat. That's why he says we "wrestle" with them. Wrestling is up close and personal. It is hand-to-hand combat.

Unlike in boxing where you can bob and weave and dance around your opponent, in wrestling you have to get close enough to put your arms around him. You have to get close enough to smell his breath. That is what Paul is saying here in this passage by using the word, "pros." It is hand-to-hand combat. Pros means "up front, close, personal contact."

So when you put these two words together, "pros" and "euche" you have the compound word "proseuchomai" meaning "a strong, desperate prayer that is leaning in towards God; in close contact with God; reaching or grasping for God; and, in a sense, putting your arms around God. This is the meaning of "pleading the case" or "prosecuting the case." Actually, you can hear the word "prosecute" in the Greek word. Prosecute. Proseuchomai.

As I began to get a grasp on this dynamic New Testament word, I was amazed to discover that almost every major prayer verse in the Bible uses a form of this word. Here are a few just to illustrate the point:

Luke 11:1—*"Lord, teach us to pray."* (Proseuchomai)

Colossians 4:2—*"Devote yourselves to prayer (*Proseuche)

Ephesians 6:18—*"Praying(Proseuchomai) with all prayer (*Proseuchomai) *and petition (* "Deesis"; to plead; to entreat; to beg), *in the Spirit…*

Luke 18:1—*"Then He spoke a parable to them, that men always ought to pray (*Proseuchomai)*, and not lose heart…"*

Philippians 4:6—*"Be anxious for nothing, but in everything by prayer (Proseuchomai) and supplication, with thanksgiving, let your requests be made known unto God."*

There are numerous verses in the Bible that portray Heaven as a Courtroom with God as the Judge, and He is urging us to come before Him and plead our case, as one might do in a courtroom.

Isaiah 41:21: *"'Present your case,' says the Lord. 'Bring forth your strong reasons,' says the King of Jacob."*

Isaiah 43:26: *"Put me in remembrance; Let us contend together; State your case, that you may be acquitted."*

Isaiah 1:18: *" Come now, and let us <u>reason</u> (to debate; to argue; to settle the matter) together, says the Lord. Though your sins are like scarlet, they shall be white as snow; though they are red like crimson, they shall be as wool."*

Hebrews 4:16: *"Let us therefore come boldly unto the throne of grace, that we may obtain mercy, and find grace to help in time of need."*

In these and other verses, God is urging us, challenging us, calling us to come before His throne and "plead the case." This is the heart of intercessory prayer. This is a different type of praying than most of us are accustomed to. This is getting one person on your heart that you desperately want to see God save, and bringing them before the throne of God again and again and again until they get saved.

This is praying with tenacity. Tenacity is the art of "not letting go." Some years ago I had a mentor in my life who was a medical doctor with a brilliant mind and an unusual boldness for Christ. When he decided to go after something, he would not rest until he got what he was after. He had a bulldog tenacity about him that I admired. One day in a phone conversation I asked him, "Do you know why a bulldog's nose is slanted backwards?" He said, "No, why?" I said, "It's so he can breathe without letting go." I said, "That describes you. You have the tenacity of a bulldog. When you get something in your mind or on your heart, you won't let it go until you get the desired result."

That is the essence of proseuchomai. That is "pleading the case." Intercessory prayer, by nature, must be bold, daring, audacious, and dangerous! That is what Jim Elliot, the martyred missionary to the Auca Indians, was referring to when he said:

> *"We are so utterly ordinary, so commonplace, while we profess to know a Power the Twentieth Century does not reckon with. But we are harmless, and therefore unharmed. We are spiritual pacifists; non-militants; conscientious objectors in this battle-to-the-death with principalities and powers in high places. Meekness must be had for contact with men, but brass, outspoken boldness is required to take part in the comradeship of the Cross. We are "sideliners"—coaching and criticizing the real wrestlers while content to sit by and leave the enemies of God unchallenged. The world cannot hate us—we are too much like its own.* **Oh, that God would make me dangerous!"**

Are you dangerous for God? Does Hell know you exist? Do you remember the seven sons of Sceva in Acts 19? They were unconverted sons of a Jewish priest, who thought they could cast out demons "by the Jesus whom Paul preaches." Verse 15 of that chapter says, *"And the evil spirit answered and said, "Jesus I know and Paul I know; but who are you?"* And you can probably guess how that story turned out. Let's just say it was not a pretty sight!

But the point I am making here, is, "Wouldn't it be something to be 'known in Hell?'" Jesus was known by the demons in Hell. Paul was known by the demons in Hell. And those who plead the case for others, depopulating Hell, rescuing those from the clutches of Satan himself, will be known in Hell.

This is also why prayer is such hard work. Have you ever noticed that? Prayer is hard work! In fact, I believe prayer is the hardest work you will ever do, because nothing you will ever do will be as opposed by Satan as interceding for the souls of others. Just ask yourself this question: "Is there anything else in my Christian life that the devil fights harder to keep me from doing than prayer?" You can do any number of things as a Christian, and there is no spiritual battle whatsoever over it. But when you begin to get serious about prayer, suddenly there are a dozen other things that pop into your mind that need to be done—right now! Do you think that is just a coincidence? Not on your life! Satan will not waste his time on things that do not matter. So the very fact that he fights prayer with everything in his arsenal ought to tell us how powerful prayer really is. So the battle is on! The prayer room is the battlefield! Satan knows he has already won the battle if he can keep you from praying. That is the power of prayer!

Think about it this way: Prayer is the only thing you can do in which you can touch three worlds at once from wherever you are. It doesn't matter if it's at a church altar, on your knees beside your bed, or under a tree somewhere. When you kneel to pray, you actually touch three worlds from that spot: The world of Heaven, the world of Earth, and the world of Hell.

First, you touch the world of **Heaven**, because God hears your prayers and will move all of Heaven, dispatching angels and heavenly hosts in order to answer your prayer.

Secondly, you touch the world of **Earth,** because when you pray, and you do it with passion and focus and energy (energeo), supernatural things happen resulting in changed lives, saved souls, healed bodies and restored marriages.

And thirdly, you touch the world of **Hell**, because when you pray, Hell trembles. Hell doesn't tremble when we have committee meetings. Hell doesn't tremble when we talk. Hell doesn't tremble when we sing or even preach, but Hell trembles when we pray.

And this is why it amazes me every time I hear some Christian say, "But I don't have time to pray!" No time to pray? Really? The average American has 27 conversations a day. We speak an average of 16,000 words a day. We have time to talk to everybody in the world and spend untold hours texting, tweeting, emailing, calling our friends, connecting on Facebook and watching TV, but we don't have time to talk to the one person in the universe who has all the power and resources to meet our every need?

We have to ask ourselves, "Do we really believe what we say we believe about God? Do we *really* believe that God has all power? Do we *really* believe that He has all knowledge? Do we know anyone else who is more connected and has more resources and wisdom than Almighty God?"

Intercession, by definition means, "to stand between." In intercessory prayer, or pleading prayer, as I like to call it, you are standing between a person in need and the only One who can meet that need, and introducing the one with the need to the One who can meet that need. It is taking the person in need with one hand and taking God with the other hand and bringing the two together.

And you are never more like Jesus when you do that because you are laying your life down for that person in need. You are bearing one another's burden. You are sharing in the suffering of Christ. And lest you think I am overstating the case of pleading in behalf of someone else, listen to Ezekiel 22:30-31:

> *"And I sought for a man among them, to make up the hedge and stand in the gap before Me for the land, that I should not destroy it. But I found none! Therefore I have poured out my indignation upon them; I have consumed them with the fire of my wrath."*

Intercession is "making up the hedge." It is "standing in the gap" for someone else.

And in Isaiah 59:16, we are astounded by the fact that God actually "wondered" about something. Think about this: What in the world could possibly make God "wonder?" Here it is:

"And He saw that there was no man, and wondered that there was no intercessor..."

Do you want to know what makes God wonder? It is the absence of intercessors. Wow! What a revelation this is! Could this be the missing element in our churches?

As God began to reveal to me the scope and power of this principle of "pleading the case," I began to see examples of it all over the Bible:

Hear Moses pleading with God not to destroy the people when they sinned and built the golden calf—and see God relent according to Moses' prayer and let the people live. (Ex. 32:1-35)

Hear Abraham pleading for God to spare Sodom and Gomorrah if he can find at least 50 righteous people, and watch as God goes with Abraham from 50 to 45 to 40 to 30 to 20 and then finally to 10 as the number to avoid judgment. (Genesis 18-19)

Hear Jacob wrestling with the angel and refusing to let go until he blesses him. And Jacob gets the blessing. I wonder how many blessings we have missed by letting go too soon! (Genesis 32:24-30)

Hear the widow pleading over and over again with the "unjust judge" in Luke 18 until she wears him down and he grants her need.

Hear the Syrophonecian Woman contending with Jesus and refusing to let her feelings stand in the way of getting her prayer answered for her daughter. (Matthew 15:21-28)

See Hannah pleading with the Lord silently in the tabernacle for a baby until Eli the Priest accuses her of being drunk. But she wasn't drunk. She was pleading with God, and Samuel was born.

Hear Isaac pleading with the Lord for his wife, Rebekah, to have a child, and see God answer his prayer as she conceived and bore twins, Jacob and Esau. (Genesis 25:21)

William and Catherine Booth, founders of the Salvation Army back in the mid-1800s, had eight children. At one point, five of them had not been saved. Catherine Booth had been praying for their salvation, and yet nothing seemed to be happening. One day in deep pleading prayer for her five unsaved children, she became rather adamant with God. In a manner, she stomped her foot and said, "God, I have five children who need to be saved, and I absolutely *refuse* to come to Heaven without all five of them! In a short time, all five had been saved!

George Mueller was perhaps the greatest prayer warrior in the last 200 years. Anyone who studies prayer will study George Mueller and how he prevailed in prayer. Mueller once said,

> *"It is not enough to begin to pray, nor to pray aright; nor is it enough to continue for a time to pray; but we must patiently, believingly, continue in prayer until we obtain an answer."*

This is the kind of praying that moves the heart of God, ushers people into the Kingdom, brings prodigal children home, breaks the hardest of hearts, and sets churches on fire. This is the kind of praying that can produce revival in the church.

One of the best things I have ever done is to get a simple prayer journal and write the names of people I would like to see saved. One by one, as I have prayed for them, I have been able to check off their names. I began with the hardest case: my own prodigal son. I had prayed for him the way most parents pray for their children for 9 years, but saw no movement toward God in his life. But after praying this way for only three months, I was blessed to get to lead my Son to Christ. The difference in his life was immediate.

Now you may be asking, "What does this really mean for me?" Well, here's what it means. It means that you can never encounter a situation about which you have to say, *"There is nothing I can do about it."* You can always pray. And prayer *is* doing something about it. As Oswald Chambers said, *"Prayer doesn't fit us for the greater work; prayer is the greater work."*

Think about it. Satan has no answer to prayer. He has no defense against it. There is no "anti-prayer" missile he can send up to stop your prayer from getting to the ear of your Heavenly Father!

The unbeliever has many defenses against our evangelistic efforts:

You can invite him to attend church with you, but he can refuse.

Even if he does show up, he can shift his mind into neutral and count the cracks in the ceiling.

You can go to his home, but he doesn't have to let you in.

You can hand him a gospel tract, but he can throw it away.

You can call him on the phone, and he can ignore you, or hang up.

You can get on TV or radio, but he can switch the channel.

But! When you pray, and pray passionately, and pray specifically, and pray with focus, he cannot prevent the Lord Jesus Christ from knocking on the door of his heart when you call his name in intercessory prayer!

Prayer is the SECRET weapon of the Christian! It is the "smart missile" of the church! So, whatever else we do, we must learn to pray, and to pray with power. And that is important for two reasons:

1. There will come a time in your life, if it hasn't already, when for God to answer your prayer will mean more to you than anything else on this earth.

2. Many of you will have loved ones and friends who are going to die and go to Hell if you don't learn how to pray effectively for the lost

I am an evangelism guy. I work in the Evangelism Office of the Alabama Baptist State Board of Missions, and I love every minute of it. I love winning souls. I have been doing it since I was 16 years old. So what I am about to say might sound strange. But I am convinced of the truth of it:

Our First Duty as Christians is **NOT** to preach the gospel! Our first Duty is **NOT** to talk to others about God. Our first duty is to be **prepared** to preach the gospel. It is to be **ready** to preach the gospel. To be so **saturated** with the Spirit of God that we are made worthy to preach the gospel, so that when we do go out and preach the gospel we are empowered with the Holy Spirit and souls get saved!

In other words, we must learn in the church today to talk to God about men before we talk to men about God! And the reason for that is because the battle for lost souls is not won on the field on evangelism. It is won in the prayer closet by prayer and intercession. Let me give you just one example from the Bible to back up what I am saying. There are others, but this one is my favorite.

Do you remember in Exodus 17:8-13 when Joshua led the Israelites in battle against the Amalekites in the Valley of Rephidim? Do you remember that Moses went up onto the mountain and lifted high the rod of God? As long as the rod of God was lifted up by Moses, the Israelites would prevail in the battle, but when his arms got tired and they began to let down, the battle shifted and the enemies of God would begin to prevail. Two men, Aaron and Hur, got on each side of Moses and held up his arms. And because his arms were held high, Israel won the battle that day. Now, here is the question: Where was the battle decided that day? In the valley with Joshua? Or on the mountain with Moses? Obviously, it was decided on the mountain with Moses! The takeaway from that story is **the victory in the valley is won by the intercession on the mountain!**

And the clear application to today is that the church of the Lord Jesus Christ could win more battles in the valley if it had more intercessors on the mountain lifting high the rod of God, the name of Jesus in prayer!

So, hear me when I say that evangelism is not the attempt to *win* the battle for souls—it is the mopping up operation after the battle has been won in the prayer closet! And the physical accouterments of the church, i.e. the buildings, organizations, committees, outreach programs and discipleship ministries are the "trucks" we drive onto the field of battle to load up the spoils of the victory won by the intercessors!

Prayer is the battlefield upon which all spiritual battles are waged. This is why Paul closes out his great warfare passage in Ephesians 6:18 with the words, "...*praying with all prayer (proseuchomai) and supplication*...."

Paul knew that prayer *is* the warfare. (6:13-17) Once you are dressed for battle, and you are standing in your spiritual armor, the place where the battle takes place is the place of prayer. The battlefield is prayer. All spiritual battles are waged on this field of prayer. The battle is won or lost here. Before we ever step onto the battlefield of evangelism, or preaching, or teaching, the outcome has already been determined on the battlefield of prayer!

There is an animal in Africa called a gnu. It is a rather unusual animal in that it has a very unique defense mechanism when attacked by another animal. When an enemy approaches a Gnu, it falls to its knees, and then suddenly leaps to attack from its knees. We need to develop a whole bunch of Gnu churches! Not NEW, but GNU! We need to learn to meet and defeat every enemy from our knees! We need to attack every adversary, defeat every difficulty, overcome every obstacle, pole vault over every problem, and hurdle over every hindrance from our knees!

In Acts 4, the early church had a prayer meeting and they discovered how to pray with power. It was *only* a prayer meeting, and yet what occurred there has been and will be commemorated for all eternity on the pages of Holy Scripture. It was *only* a prayer meeting, but the fire fell, and house was shaken, and their lives were shaken, and the city was shaken, and the truths continue to shake us today! It may only be a prayer meeting, but who knows what God might do when His people gather for powerful, passionate, pleading prayer!

Go back and reread the opening paragraph of this chapter. Almost as a direct confirmation of the truth of those statements, someone sent me today an article published by Baptist Press about the Revival that is taking place at Long Hollow Baptist Church in Hendersonville, Tennessee. The heading of the article states: **"Long Hollow revival steeped in prayer sees 1,000 baptisms since December."** Did you hear that? "...**revival, steeped in prayer...1,000 baptisms"** There is the key!

The picture under that heading is of a former Satan worshipper who recently gave his life to Christ baptizing his friend, Patricia, another former Satan worshipper on December 20, 2020. This marked a wave of baptisms that exceeded 1,000 on April, 11, 2021. The church has focused on prayer and made spontaneous baptisms a part of the fabric of their church. Pastor Robby Gallaty made the statement in the article that *"The Lord has shown me that prayer births revival, and revival births prayer. It's like adding logs to the fire."* Indeed, prayer must precede revival, and prayer will sustain revival.

With that thought in mind, I will close this rather lengthy chapter with a story from R.A. Torrey, who was D.L. Moody's successor:

> *"Up in a little town in Maine, things were pretty dead some years ago. The churches were not accomplishing anything. There were a few godly men in the churches, and they said: "Here we are, only uneducated laymen; but something must be done in this town. Let us form a praying band. We will all center our prayers on one man. Who shall it be?" They picked out one of the hardest men in town, a hopeless drunkard, and centered all their prayers upon him. In a week, he was converted. They centered their prayers upon the next hardest man in town, and soon he was converted. Then they took up another and another; until within a year, two or three hundred were brought to God, and fire spread out into all the surrounding country. Definite prayer for those in the prison house of sin is the need of the hour!"*

150 years later, I couldn't agree more! Pastors, whatever else we do, let us teach our people to pray!

10

CHARACTERISTIC # 7 THE WORD

A NEW DELIGHT IN THE WORD OF GOD

"Scripture is the manger in which Christ lies. As a mother goes to a cradle to find her baby, so the Christian goes to the Bible to find Jesus."
---Martin Luther

"If Jesus preached the same message ministers preach today, He never would have been crucified."
--Leonard Ravenhill

When the fire falls, the Bible becomes precious to the believer. When the Spirit is poured out upon a people in genuine revival, believers begin to delight in the Word of God as never before. They will cling to His Word. They will cherish His Word. They will hungrily seek His Word. The Bible "comes alive" and the Word becomes real as revived believers discover new insights in the Word, and God's voice becomes clear as he speaks through the Word.

I have never experienced a personal revival that it did not lead me into a deeper love and appreciation for the Word of God. It is axiomatic. Genuine revival will always lead you deeper into God's Word.

The Precious Book

Though the cover is torn, and the pages are worn,
And though places bear traces of tears,
Yet more precious than gold is the book worn and old
That can shatter and scatter my fears.

When I prayerfully look in the precious old book,
Many pleasures and treasures I see,
Many tokens of love from the Father above
That is nearest and dearest to me.

This old book's been my guide; Tis a friend by my side,
It will lighten and brighten my way
And each new promise I find, soothes and gladdens my mind
As I read it and heed it today.

When revival broke out on the campus of Wheaton College in the mid 1990's, Dr. Timothy K. Beougher was the Assistant Professor of Evangelism. He recounts arriving at Pierce Chapel on Monday evening at about 8:45 pm to pray and reflect on what was happening on the campus of this evangelical college. Then he noticed something unusual.

He said, "Students began pouring into the auditorium at about 9:15 pm. Immediately I was struck by the fact that many of them were carrying Bibles. Wheaton students have Bibles, but they don't always bring them to meetings. Yet student after student walked in with a Bible. It suddenly hit me—this was one of Jonathan Edwards' "Distinguishing Marks of a Work of the Spirit of God"! Edwards penned this classic work during the First Great Awakening (1741) to help people distinguish a genuine work of God from mere emotionalism. I retraced in my mind Edward's five distinguishing marks of a genuine work of God:

1. It raises the esteem of Jesus.

2. Satan's kingdom suffers as the Spirit of God strikes out against sin.

3. Men and women will have a greater respect for Scripture.

4. Men and women will see more clearly spiritual truth and error.

5. There will be a new sense of love toward God and others.

I sat in quiet gratitude as I reflected on what I had seen on our campus and how it mirrored these marks of revival as delineated by Jonathan Edwards."

It is that third characteristic of revival Edwards mentions that I am zeroing in on now. The Bible must be central in revival. When God's Spirit is poured out in revival, the Word is exalted and authoritative over man's experience. Many of our "so-called" revivals today center around human experience and emotion, rather than the authority of God's Word. Richard Owens Roberts, one of the most competent authorities on revival, distinguishes the difference between *Word-centered* revivals and *experience-centered* revivals. He says, "The Bible will play a major role in any genuine revival, as will emotion. The question is which will be most prominent."

Dr. Roy Fish used to teach that "The Word-centered revival is much more prone to last because Bible teaching and preaching take precedence. Experience-centered revivals are usually brief. The Word-centered revival of 1800 lasted forty years. The more experience-centered Welsh revival did a great deal of good, but it was over in two years."

It has been said that where there is fire, there is always a danger of wildfire. So it is with many of the experience-centered revivals. I call them pseudo revivals. There is very little Word, and a whole lot of "experiences." Many of them border on the bizarre and absurd. There is no such thing as a biblical revival that starts with "Holy Laughter," crawling around on all fours barking like dogs and howling like wolves, or stumbling around like you're drunk as in the so-called "Laughing Revival." Hell laughs at such a thought while Heaven weeps!

Why in the world are we so obsessed today with fads like "gold dust" falling from the ceiling, "glory clouds," and "angel feathers"? I am disturbed by the "westernization of Christianity" and the lack of discernment in the 21st century church! Could it be that we are so biblically illiterate that we have become modern day fulfillments of P.T. Barnum's famous statement, "There is a sucker born every minute"? I actually believe that the reason we fall for every trick of the hucksters and peddlers of God's Word is because we do not believe the Word of God is powerful enough to change people's lives. We think the Gospel needs some additives to help it sputter along.

When will we ever learn that the Holy Scriptures are completely and entirely sufficient and they will never lead us to silliness, foolishness, and frivolity. To elevate man's ideas and experiences above the Word of God is to become vulnerable to confusion and error. We become easy prey for the one who is the Master Counterfeiter. It is a grave error to think of revival only in terms of joy and ecstasy, exuberant rejoicing and singing praises to God. But unfortunately, isn't that what we normally think of when we think of revival? Dr. J. Edwin Orr used to say, "When we pray for revival, most of us don't have any idea what we are praying for. We think we are praying for ecstasy—and yes, joy is a by-product of revival—*but revival does not begin in ecstasy, but in agony."*

Almost all of the revivals in history began when God's people became desperate for Him, and they were driven to His Word by their desperation. The Word then brought about conviction, contrition, and repentance, and revival was the result. The greatest revival in history was the Protestant Reformation, which was born out of the desperation of Martin Luther's soul as he tried to find forgiveness for his sins. One day as he was studying the book of Romans he stumbled across Romans 1:17, "The Just shall live by faith." His eyes were opened to the truth that salvation comes by grace rather than works, and the Protestant Reformation was born. Revival is always birthed out of the Word of God, and it is also sustained by the Word of God.

When God's people are revived and the Spirit is poured out upon them, they will delight in His Word. Above personalities. Above experiences. Above the most current fads and gimmicks. They will cherish His Word and they will seek after His Word with a hunger to know more about God and His holiness. And for all that, it will not be an exercise for information about God's Word, but rather a heart-felt seeking of God's Word to learn more about the God who has saved them.

I heard the story about an old Indian chief back in the 1800's who had been pushed further and further West until he and his tribe came to a mountain. The old chief was tired, so he called three of his best warriors together and told them, "I want you to go up to the mountain and see what's on the other side. We will camp here until you come back. Pick up some rocks and tokens of the things that you find on the other side." They were gone for several days, and when they returned they had nothing in their hands. The chief said, "Where are the rocks and tokens of the things on the other side of the mountain you were supposed to bring back?" With wide-eyed amazement, they exclaimed, *"We saw the sea!"*

Many Christians spend their life going from one experience to another, seeking this sign or another, gathering autographs from this Christian celebrity or another, but when you open up God's Word and see Christ and His cross---you've seen the sea!

And once you've seen the sea—all the other little things that you thought were noteworthy and important become nothing more than rocks and tokens that you picked up along the way. Why be satisfied with rocks and tokens, when God wants to show you the vastness of the sea?

This is what the Apostle Paul was referring to when he said in Philippians 3:10: *"That I may know Him, and the power of His resurrection, and the fellowship of His sufferings, being made conformable to His death."*

"That I may know Him…." This was Paul's goal in life once he "saw the sea." He wanted to plumb the depths of who God was. He wanted to know Him deeply, personally, intimately. *"For me to live, is Christ, and to die is gain."*(Phil. 1:21) There was nothing else worth living for once he found Christ.

> *"Yet indeed I also count all things loss for the excellence of the knowledge of Christ Jesus my Lord, for whom I have suffered the loss of all things, and count them as rubbish, that I may gain Christ."* (Phil. 3:8)

This passion to know Christ led Paul to a deep study of His Word until after dealing extensively with the majestic subject of the Sovereignty of God in Romans 9-11, it's as though he drops to his knees, lifts his hands into the air, and exclaims, *"Oh the depth of the riches, both of the wisdom and knowledge of God! How unsearchable are His judgments and His ways past finding out!"* (Romans 11:33)

And how incredibly deep the Word of God is! It is unfathomable! Freejof Nanson explored the Arctic. He was a Norwegian. He did not have the depth finders and the things that modern explorers have, so when he got to the Arctic region, Freejof Nanson let down a rope to see how deep it was. And the fathom did not hit the bottom, so he put in his ship's log, "deeper than that." The next day, he doubled the rope and let it down, and still he did not touch bottom. And he wrote in the ship's log, "deeper than that." The next day, he took all of the rope that he had on board the ship and tied it together and let it down. Still it didn't touch the bottom, and he wrote in his ship's log, "deeper than that." That's how it is with the Word of God! You can let out all the rope in your mind and you'll never plumb the depths of God's Word. It is "deeper than that." You can exhaust all your energy studying it, and you'll never touch the bottom of the Word. It is "deeper than that." You can go to seminary and earn Bible degrees to study the Bible until you have more degrees than a thermometer, and still never plumb the depths of God's Holy Word. It is "deeper than that."

David said in Psalm 92:5, "Oh Lord, thy thoughts are very deep." After he had been preaching for 40 years, Charles Spurgeon said,

> *"Nobody ever out-grows the Scripture. The book widens and deepens with our years. Brethren, it is inexhaustible! A long life will only suffice to skirt the shores of this great continent of light. The Word is like its author, infinite, immeasurable, and without end."*

Billy Sunday was a major league baseball player turned evangelist in the 1880's. He was fiery and controversial. It was Billy Sunday who coined the phrase, "Walk the Sawdust Trail" in reference to people coming to be saved in his tent revivals walking on ground covered in sawdust. He wrote one of the most moving tributes to the Bible:

> *"Twenty-nine years ago, with the Holy Spirit as my guide, I entered the wonderful temple Christianity. I entered at the portico of Genesis, walked down through the Old Testament art galleries where pictures of Noah, Abraham, Isaac, Jacob, Joseph, Moses, and Daniel are hung on the wall.*
>
> *I passed into the music room of Psalms where the Spirit swept the keyboard of my nature until it seemed that every reed and pipe of God's great organ responded to the tuneful harp of David, the sweet singer of Israel.*
>
> *I entered the chamber of Ecclesiastes where the voice of the preacher was heard, and into the conservatory of Sharon where the Lily of the Valley's sweet-scented spices filled and perfumed my life.*
>
> *I entered into the business office of Proverbs, and then into the observatory room of the prophets where I saw telescopes of various sizes pointed to far off events, but all concentrated on the Bright and Morning Star, which is the King of Kings.*
>
> *I caught a vision of His glory from the standpoint of Matthew, Mark, Luke, and John, and passed into the Acts of the Apostles where the Holy Spirit was doing His work in the formation of the infant Church. Then into the*

> *correspondence room where sat Paul, Peter, James and John penning their epistles.*
>
> *I stepped into the throne room of Revelation, where towered the glittering peaks, and caught a vision of the King sitting upon the throne in all His glory. And I cried, "All hail the power of Jesus' name! Let angels prostrate fall! Bring forth the royal diadem and crown Him Lord of all!"*

That's the kind of preaching we need today. Preaching that is steeped in Scripture and centered on Christ! Whatever else you may think you are, pastor, let me remind you once again that you are first and foremost a preacher of the Word of God. So, preach the Word! Your church may overlook a lot of things and forgive you for a lot of mistakes, but one thing they will not overlook, nor forgive you for, is a failure to feed them from the Word of God. Preach the Bible, and let every sermon lift up Jesus Christ! Let me once again quote Charles Spurgeon who said,

> *"A sermon without Christ as its beginning, middle, and end is a mistake in conception and a crime in execution…If any man can preach one sermon without mentioning Christ's name in it, it ought to be his last, certainly the last that any Christian ought to go to hear him preach… When we preach Christ crucified, we have no reason to stammer, or stutter, or hesitate or apologize; there is nothing in the gospel of which we have any cause to be ashamed."*

The problem today is that our churches are majoring on minors and minoring on majors. We have become hungry for everything but the Word in these troubled times. I agree with Michael Catt who says, "Too many sermons today are too full of illustrations, much like a house made of glass. Impressive, but not where you want to be in a storm. Revival preaching has to be a return to Scripture—line by line, precept upon precept, text in context."

We do not need to hear men's opinions. We need to hear, "Thus saith the Lord!" My mentor back in the 90's once said to me, "Your opinion and my opinion are of equal value. And your opinion is absolutely worthless and totally irrelevant!" At first, I wanted to be offended, until I realized what he was saying. He was saying that my opinion and his were of equal value and neither one really mattered. The only thing that really matters is what God says!

I am 100% convinced that if we are going to see revival today, we are going to have to have a baptism of courage and boldness in the pulpits across this nation to preach more than human opinions. We need men in the pulpit who will preach the truth, the whole truth, and nothing but the truth. Erwin Lutzer says, *"In a time of universal deception, telling the truth is a revolutionary act."* I believe we are living in that time, and more than ever, we need men of God who are willing to tell the truth!

This is not a time for dilly dallying or tiptoeing through the tulips. We need to immerse ourselves in the Word of God and the history of revival so that we know how to respond to the coming tide of evil that is even now flooding our land. As one of my pastor friends said to me just this week, "I don't think we are far away from having to go underground as the church in America." We need to focus on what God has said and what God has done in the past in order to know what we must do to see revival in our day. Revival doesn't come through sports programs, food relief ministries, committee meetings, or Sunday School classes. All these are good, but nothing can ever take the place of the Word of God. True revival springs up from the Word of God. I still believe that when a man of God will get filled with the Spirit of God, bury his heart and mind in the Word of God, stand up in the house of God, open the Word of God, and preach the truth of God, to the people of God, with the anointing of God, the Holy Spirit of God will be poured out upon the church of God and revival will be on!

We are living in difficult days. Perilous times. We are witnessing what began as a cultural shift, but now has become a cultural landslide. Most Christians are paralyzed with fear and confusion as they watch the last remaining vestiges of the moral foundation of our country being torn away. Marxism continues its march of aggression across the landscape of our nation as Christians are bullied into silence by fear of accusations of "systemic racism," "white privilege," and "intolerance." But where are the prophets of our day? Why are our pulpits silent? Do we have puppets in our pulpits or prophets? We don't need cute or clever, we need courage and conviction!

A.W. Tozer said,

> *"We who preach the gospel must not think of ourselves as public relations agents sent to establish good will between Christ and the world. We must not imagine ourselves commissioned to make Christ acceptable to big business, the press, the world of sports, or modern education. We are not diplomats, but prophets, and our message is not a compromise, but an ultimatum."*

No revival has ever taken place in the absence of a prophet. God has always had His prophet to call God's people out of complacency and idolatry before Revival can come. Without a prophet, God's people will be content with religion. Without a prophet God's people will be satisfied with their sins and with the status quo. Without a prophet, the church buildings may be full, but the altars will be empty. In his deeply convicting book, <u>America is too Young to Die</u>, Leonard Ravenhill said:

> *"There is a terrible vacuum in evangelical Christianity today. The missing person in our ranks is the prophet. The man with the terrible earnestness. The man totally other worldly. The man rejected by other men, even other good men, because they consider him too austere, too severely committed, too negative and unsociable."*

The prophet Amos made a prediction that should have shaken all of Israel to the core of their being. He said, *"'Behold, the days are coming,'" declares the Lord God, "'When I will send a famine on the land, not a famine for bread, or a thirst for water, but rather for hearing the words of the Lord.'"* (Amos 8:11). That prophecy came true shortly after Malachi prophesied. There were 400 years that God did not speak from Heaven. We call that the "400 silent years." We are experiencing a famine of the Word of God today also. Leonard Ravenhill also says:

> *"Just a couple of days ago a fine preacher brother said to me, 'We have no great preachers in the country anymore.' I think I know what he meant: no outstanding man with a 'thus saith the Lord,' a man terrible in utterance under the anointing of the Spirit. We have gifted preachers, talented preachers, orator preachers, famous preachers, organizing preachers, but where, oh where, are the preachers who startle the nation with prophetic utterance? There is a famine of great preaching, a famine of strong expository preaching, a famine of conscience-stirring preaching, a famine of heartbreaking preaching, a famine of soul-stirring preaching, a famine of that preaching like our fathers knew which kept men awake all night lest they fall into hell. I repeat, 'There is a famine of the word of the Lord.'"*

Maybe you're thinking, "How do I encourage my pastor to get into the Word of God like that? How can I help him make preaching a priority? How can I pray for him to get a burden from the Lord and the boldness to preach like a prophet?

If you had been at the 1990 Southern Baptist Convention Pastor's Conference in New Orleans, LA, you would have heard Dr. John McArthur answer that question in one of the most powerful challenges for preachers to become men of God you could ever hear. Here is what he said churches should do to help their pastor become a man of the Word:

> *"Fling him into his office, then tear the 'Office' sign from the door, and replace it with a sign that says, "Study." Take him off the mailing list. Lock him up with his books and his computer and his Bible. Slam him down on his knees before texts and broken hearts, a sometimes-superficial flock and a holy God. Force him to be the one man in the community who knows about God. Throw him into the ring to box with God until he learns how short his arms are. Engage him to wrestle with God all the night through and let him come out only when he's bruised and beaten into being a blessing. Shut his mouth from forever spouting remarks and stop his tongue from forever tripping lightly over every non-essential. Require him to have something to say before he breaks the silence. Burn his eyes with weary study. Wreck his emotional poise with worry for the things of God. Rip out his telephone. Burn up his success sheets. Put water in his gas tank. Give him a Bible and tie him to the pulpit. Test him,*

*quiz him, examine him. Humiliate him for his ignorance of things divine. Shame him for his good comprehension of finance, batting averages, and political party issues. Laugh at his frustrated effort to play psychiatrist. Form a choir, raise a chant and haunt him night and day with, 'Sir, we would know God.' When at long last he does ascend the pulpit, ask him if he has a word from God. If he doesn't, then dismiss him. Tell him you can read the paper. You can digest the television commentary. You can think through the day's superficial problems and manage the weary drives of the community and bless the assorted baked potatoes and green beans better than he can. And when he does speak God's Word, listen. And when he's burned out finally by the flaming Word, consumed by the fiery grace blazing through him, and when he's privileged to translate the truth of God to man and finally is himself transferred from earth to heaven, bear him away gently. Blow a muted trumpet. Lay him down softly and place a two-edged sword on his coffin and raise the tune triumphant, for ere he died he had become a **Man of God.**"*

When genuine revival comes, it always produces a new delight in the Word of God!

11

CHARACTERISTIC # 8 WORSHIP

A PURER AND MORE PASSIONATE WORSHIP

> *"I need to worship because without it I can forget that I have a big God beside me and live in fear. I need to worship because without it I can forget his calling and begin to live in a spirit of self-preoccupation. I need to worship because without it I lose a sense of wonder and gratitude and plod through life with blinders on. I need worship because my natural tendency is toward self-reliance and stubborn independence."*
> --John Ortberg

In seasons of revival, worship takes on a new dynamic. Our hearts are thoroughly right with God, the Spirit is being poured out, and joy-filled believers want to sing and worship God with a newfound freedom.

I am always perplexed when I preach in revival meetings at how many church members just stand there without making any effort to sing. This seems to be especially true of men. Why do men find it difficult to sing in church? I vividly remember back in the 1990's seeing men at Promise Keepers wearing shirts that said, *"Real* men sing, *real* loud!" I laughed out loud when I first saw that, but I *really* like that saying. I think men ought to sing, if for no other reason than to let their children and grandchildren hear them singing God's praises without shame! It has been my experience that in times of revival, *real* men are not ashamed to sing *real* loud.

The Psalmist said in Psalm 27:4-6,

> *"One thing I have desired of the Lord, and that will I seek; that I may dwell in the house of the Lord all the days of my life, to behold the beauty of the Lord and to inquire in His temple. For in the time of trouble He shall hide me in His pavilion; in the secret place of His tabernacle He shall hide me; He shall set me high upon a rock. And now shall my head be lifted up above my enemies all around me; Therefore I will offer sacrifices of joy in His tabernacle; I will sing, yes, I will sing praises to the Lord."*

And in Psalm 57: 7 he said, *"My heart is fixed, O Lord, my heart is fixed. I will sing and give praise!"*

The Psalms are saturated with the spirit of praise. Just read Psalm 30 or Psalm 40, or Psalm 42 or Psalm 95 and you'll see that David knew how to praise God in every circumstance of life. So when I am feeling down or discouraged, I turn to the Psalms. You simply cannot walk with David through the Psalms without being encouraged and feeling revived.

Singing sounds different during times of revival. Worship looks different during times of revival. Tears flow freely. People aren't afraid to express their love for Jesus. And the people of God want to worship. They cannot help but worship. Worship and revival go hand in hand as evidenced by a testimony of the Welch Revival that I recently heard. The narrator of the story is unknown, but the story is powerful nonetheless:

> *"I met our brother here in a Welch town called Dullos. Dullos is up the tracks from our village about six miles. I worked with a lot of men in the coalmines near Dullos. They were nearly all from Dullos, the fellows that I worked with.*

WHEN THE FIRE FALLS

Let me tell you a little story about Dullos. It's how the Welch revival came to our village. The schoolmaster in our village was a man by the name of T.C. Thomas. This was in 1904. He heard that the great Welch revivalist, Evan Roberts, was in Dullos. So after school one evening he went up to Dullos, and like everyone else, caught fire. You just could not go into those revival meetings without catching fire! After the service was over, he came down on the Coal Miners' train and he got into the village about a quarter till ten.

Now, I don't know if it's the same now, but at ten o'clock all the taverns closed. I think it might be a little later now, but at ten o'clock all the taverns closed. He came off the train at the railway station; the railway depot, but he was so filled with God that he couldn't go home. He wore a silk top hat and silk tails and a silver knobbed cane, and he got off the train, came out of the railroad station, and right there on the road, he took off his hat and laid down his cane, got down on his knees and began to sing the praises of God.

You see, we will learn perhaps better one day that all the world moves on music; on sound impulses; on music, and what a great thing it is to express the things of God in music. The Apostle Paul said that one of the great signs of being filled with the Holy Spirit is singing to yourselves; not speaking to yourselves, but singing to yourselves in Psalms and hymns and spiritual songs. He's put a song in our hearts.

And so my grandmother was coming up the hill from the bottom of the village, with a friend of hers that we got to know very well, Mrs. Naomi George, and they were coming up and they heard this singing, but they couldn't tell where it was coming from. And so she went to the janitor of the church there, the Church of England, again, a dear old lady that I knew in later years, a Mrs. Bernal, and she said to her, 'Mrs. Bernal, you've locked the vicar in the church!' And Mrs. Bernal said, 'Never!' And she said, 'Oh yes! We can hear him singing!'

And so Mrs. Bernal got the key and went to the Church of England, which, of course was also the Church of Wales, but the Church of England, and there was no vicar in the church. And they could hear this singing, coming from nowhere, but coming for everywhere! You see, just 50 yards below where T.C. Thomas was singing was the station hotel and tavern. And the men heard him singing. You've never really heard hymn singing until you've heard a bunch of Welchmen outside a tavern singing!

Someone said, 'T.C. Thomas has gone mad! He's on his knees up there singing!' And some of them with their glasses in their hand went up and they stood around poor old T.C. Thomas, and there he was with tears streaming down his face and his hands up to God singing. Now all Welch hymnology is packed full of the blood of Jesus Christ! And he was singing and magnifying the blood of Jesus. And you know, just 15 yards away was Sammy's Billiard Hall. I've played Billiards in Sammy's many times! And the fellows looked out of the window and they said, 'T.C. Thomas is going mad!' So they put down their billiard cues and came out and some of them still had their cues in their hand. And they stood around poor old T.C. Thomas and now here they were from the station hotel; here they were from Sammy's Billiard Hall. It was only a quarter till ten that night, and some of the women came out, and strange things began to happen.

T.C. Thomas was quite unaware of any of them being there. He was praising God! And then suddenly one man with a beer glass in his hand, got down on his knees, and began to join with T.C. Thomas, and then another, and another, until by the time my grandmother came up the hill there were dozens of men, some of them with beer glasses in their hand, some of them with billiard cues in their hands; housewives with their aprons on, falling on their knees. And that night, scores of people gave their hearts to Christ with not a preacher near them! The Holy Spirit was falling! Singing and praising and magnifying Jesus Christ!

You know there's a Scottish chorus; it's a prayer that says, 'Once more, Lord, once more, as in the days of Yore. On this dear land, Thy Spirit fall, Set Scotland now on fire.' Wouldn't it be great if men and women of all communions; it doesn't matter what; began to sing:

'Once more, Lord, once more

As in the Days of Yore,

On this dear land, Thy Spirit fall,

Set America now on fire.'

That's how the revival came to our village."

The Welch Revival was a revival of worship. In 1904 it was not unusual for people to fill up the village church with literally no one to lead the service. After a while someone would stand and give a testimony or sing a hymn of worship and in a matter of moments with the people singing and worshipping God, the Spirit of God would fall upon the congregation and revival would come with many being saved.

On one occasion, after the building was full, and the people were waiting before the Lord, an older gentleman stood and began to sing the Hymn, "Here is Love, vast as the Ocean." It was the favorite hymn of the Welch revival and became known as "The Love Song of the Welch Revival." It wasn't a song about all the miracles taking place, but about the love of Christ and his sacrifice upon the Cross.

I will never forget the first time I heard it sung in the Gaelic language and then in English. I was so moved by the lyrics and the beautiful melody. I fell in love with it and have been singing it ever since. It is absolutely one of the most beautiful hymns I have ever heard. Read the words slowly and hear heaven's echo in this "love song of the Welch Revival":

HERE IS LOVE, VAST AS THE OCEAN

> Here is love, vast as the ocean,
> Loving-kindness as the flood,
> When the Prince of Life, our Ransom,
> Shed for us His precious blood.
> Who His love will not remember?
> Who can cease to sing His praise?
> He can never be forgotten,
> Throughout Heaven's eternal days.
>
> On the Mount of crucifixion,

Fountains opened deep and wide;
Through the floodgates of God's mercy
Flowed a vast and gracious tide,
Grace and love, like mighty rivers,
Poured incessant from above,
Heaven's peace and perfect justice,
Kissed a guilty world in love.
Let me all Thy love accepting,
Love Thee, ever all my days;
Let me seek Thy kingdom only,
And my life be to Thy praise.
Thou alone shall be my glory,
Nothing in the world I see.
Thou hast cleansed and sanctified me,
Thou Thyself hast set me free.

In Thy truth Thou dost direct me,
By Thy Spirit through Thy Word;
And Thy grace my need is meeting,
As I trust in Thee, my Lord,
Of Thy fullness Thou art pouring
Thy great love and power on me,
Without measure, full and boundless,
Drawing out my heart to Thee."

I'm afraid that many, if not most, of our churches have forgotten what worship really is. Worship is not just singing songs in church. Worship is not "the preliminary to the main event." Worship is not three hymns and a poem. Worship is the highest and noblest act a person can engage in whereby he gives himself over to God in total surrender and praise because of who He is and what He has done for us in Jesus Christ.

Worship is "the missing jewel of the church today." This phrase was coined by a preacher back in 1961. A group of ministers had gathered for a special series of meetings in Canada, and they had invited one of their favorite preachers, a man by the name of A.W. Tozer, to speak. Here is the report of what happened:

> *"He was not a physically impressive individual or one known for his charisma and eloquence. But he was a man who knew God, and walked closely with Him. When he stood before that group of ministers and announced his subject, they were shocked, because the topic he chose was 'Worship.' And in this message, he made the statement, 'Worship is the missing jewel of the evangelical church.' They, being ministers, were shocked at this topic because thought they knew pretty much all there was to know about that subject. After all, that was their forte'; their craft. What else was there to learn about it? But 'learn' they did! Those messages were so powerful and life changing that they were published in a booklet and are still available today, as are most of A.W. Tozer's works."*

This one statement, "Worship is the missing jewel of the evangelical church" is as meaningful today as it was the day he first said it, and maybe even more so. And although that was 60 years ago, I'm afraid the jewel in most of our churches and in most places of the world, is still missing.

You can tell if a church is in revival from the first verse of the first song that is sung in a service. Is the song alive? Are the people singing from their hearts, or just mumbling the words for fear of someone hearing them singing? Is there energy on the platform, but none in the pews? Is the congregation simply watching the musicians perform, or are they enthusiastically participating in the service?

In the early days of the church, the services were spontaneous, Spirit filled, and participatory. Believers overflowed with love for their Savior and let it be known in their singing. James A. Stewart, a great author on revival, said, of the early church,

> *"Their whole life was flooded with praise. The assembly gatherings were characterized with praise. They praised God for His glorious salvation. They praised Him that they were counted worthy to be ambassadors of the Lord*

> *Jesus. They praised Him that they could suffer shame and reproach for His glory. They praised Him that they had something to sacrifice for the spread of the gospel. Deep spirituality and worship go hand in hand. Read the hymns of the past centuries...the saints bursting forth spontaneously into songs of adoration and worship is one of the glories of revival."*

In genuine revival, the heart is cleansed from sin and filled with love for God. Worship is the overflow of a heart that is full of God. Alfred P. Gibbs wrote in his excellent book entitled, "Worship:"

"Broadly speaking, prayer is the occupation of the soul with its needs. Praise is the occupation of the soul with its blessings. Worship is the occupation of the soul with God Himself."

Notice what he said worship is. *"It is occupation of the soul with God Himself."*

You are not worshipping when you are looking at your watch and anxious to get out of the service. You are not worshipping when your mind is on what you are going to do this afternoon or what you have to get done next week. If your mind is on anything but God, you are not and cannot worship, for worship is when your mind and your heart is focused on God.

Gibbs goes on to say to say of worship,

> *"It is not something which has to be laboriously pumped up, but that which springs up, and overflows from a heart filled with a sense of the greatness and goodness of God."*

The Psalmist says in Psalm 45:1, *"My heart is overflowing with a good theme..."* The marginal rendering of this phrase is, *"My heart boileth, or bubbleth up."* As the Psalmist meditated on the glory and majesty of God, his heart began to warm within him, until it boiled over in worship and praise to God!

You see, worship is God's idea. Anthropologists have told us that man is incurably religious. Every civilization that has ever been discovered has worshipped something. So this is obviously God's doing. God placed within man's heart an insatiable desire to worship. The only question is, *what*, or *who* will we worship? Augustine said, *"There is a divine restlessness within the heart of every man that will not be satisfied until it brings him to God."*

The Bible opens in Genesis with a worship service as Adam and Eve walked and talked with God in the Garden. In Genesis 4:1-4 we see the first formal worship service. There were two men. And two offerings. They both brought an offering to God. And we learn in this story that there are ways to get to God that are unacceptable to Him. They were both sincere. Yet sincerity is not the issue. Acceptability is the issue. We do not come to God on our terms. We come to God on His terms. And God had taught Adam about blood sacrifice, and Adam had taught his sons. But Cain decided that he had a better way to worship. We learn from the story, however, that his way was unacceptable. And it led to the first death in the Bible. Proverbs 14:12 says, *"There is a way that seems right to a man, but its end is the way of death."*

Did you know that if you turn to the middle of the Bible, you turn to that body of Wisdom literature that is called the Psalms. This was the Hebrew Baptist Hymnal! The Psalms are worship songs to God. Isn't it interesting that the Bible opens up with a worship service. In the middle is a book that gives us the stuff of worship. And it concludes in a worship service in heaven. (Revelation 19:1-16) That tells me that worship holds a very special place in our Heavenly Father's heart. That being the case, it should hold a very special place in our hearts too.

See, I don't know about you, but I confess that I have a problem. It's expressed in the great hymn, "Come Thou Fount of Every Blessing." It says, "Prone to wander, Lord, I feel it. Prone to leave the God I love." Here is my problem. I still sin. I hate it, but I do. I do not believe I will ever walk away from Jesus (although I remember another who said that—Simon Peter). But here's the thing. If I ever did walk away, it probably wouldn't be a sermon that would bring me back. I think I could handle sermons. But what I couldn't handle would be the hymns! They would break me! The great hymns of the faith are most likely what would tear down my resistance and break my rebellious heart. They can move me in the deepest part of my soul and quickly put me on my face before God.

By the way, I believe that is the highest posture of worship. On my face before Almighty God! Have you ever noticed in the book of Revelation how many times John falls down before Jesus? He just keeps falling down on his face in worship. And, in contrast, have you ever noticed how people on TV fall when the televangelist "slays them in the Spirit"? They always fall backward. With Jesus, John was always falling on his face. (Revelation 1:17; 19:10; 22:8) But when these televangelists do it, they are falling backward. Give that some thought.

The Bible tells us to *"Humble yourselves in the sight of God, and He will lift you up."* (James 4:10) Now there are very few ways one can physically humble himself. Kneeling, or bowing, or laying prostrate are ways you can do that.

In the Hebrew idiom, the foot was always the symbol of "self-will" (Eccl. 5:1). In Isaiah 6, the Seraphim covered their feet with their wings in order to avoid being self-willed and thereby to avoid rebellion to God.

In kneeling before the Lord in worship, man yields his will to God. So, when a man kneels, he is literally taking himself off his feet, thus surrendering his will to the One to Whom he kneels.

In the bowing of the head in worship, man confesses his humility in the presence of Holy God.

In closing his eyes in worship, man confesses his reverence for God, admitting that if he looked into the face of God, he would be destroyed. He is blocking out everything and anything else so he can focus totally and wholly upon God.

In the lifting up of the hands in worship, the self is symbolically lifted to God in an act of sacrifice and worship.

In the bowing of the face to the ground, all of the above are accomplished in one action, all of which demonstrates a heart of worship.

Have you ever been in a worship service where the very atmosphere seemed to be charged with the power of the Holy Spirit? Where the presence of God was palpable? Where the worship was so powerful, the Spirit was so real, that all you could do is stand there and cry? And you felt like you could reach out your hand and touch Him? Have you ever been so caught up in the moment that you felt like at any moment you could be transported to the very throne room of Heaven, and nothing else mattered except pouring your heart out to God in adoration and worship? Those moments of true worship leave you with a desire for more of Jesus. More of God. You wish it could go on forever. Well, that's what I think worship in Heaven will be like. And the closest thing to that we can come to on this earth when we experience times of personal or corporate revival. And oh! How we need more of that in our lives.

So, whatever else may happen when genuine revival comes, one thing will inevitably happen--God's people will come before Him in a spirit of humble, passionate, pure and heartfelt, worship.

12

CHARACTERISTIC # 9 SOULWINNING

SPONTANEOUS AND JOYFUL SHARING OF THE GOSPEL

"Lord, help me be a <u>nobody</u>, who will tell <u>everybody</u> about <u>Somebody</u> who can save <u>anybody</u>."
--The Soulwinner's Prayer

History bears witness that more souls are ushered into the Kingdom of God during seasons of revival than at any other time. When God comes in revival, evangelism rises to the top like cream.

I can remember when I was called as pastor to my first church in Pascagoula, Mississippi. I was 23 years old and my wife was six months pregnant with our first child. I knew nothing about pastoring a church at that tender young age; in fact, I knew very little about *anything* at that time in my life! But I did know the Gospel, and I did know that winning souls was the most important thing you could do in this life. I still believe that with all my heart. My church averaged about 33 people in attendance, mostly older adults with a few middle-aged folks and hardly any youth or children.

After I had been there a few weeks, I asked my daddy, who was a pretty good carpenter, to build a set of prayer benches for the front of our sanctuary. He built two beautiful altars, with nice blue padding on the top, painted an off-white color to match our pews, and on the day he delivered them to our church, he looked over at me and said, "Well, son, I'll tell you one thing, you've definitely got your work cut out for you if you're going to see this church grow." I knew what he was saying was true because we were in a terrible location for a church, and I had read some of the history of the church. It was not very encouraging, to say the least.

Several older pastors had warned me not to go there. One told me that I should go there for a year or two just to get some pastoral experience and then move on to a better church. He said, "But don't expect it to grow. That church has been sitting there for years and it hasn't grown at all. Another pastor went so far as to say that if I went there it would probably ruin my ministry. I didn't want to ignore their "seasoned" counsel, but there was one problem: God was telling me to go.

It had been a year and a half since they had baptized anyone in that church. The baptistry had not been used in so long that it was full of spider webs and wood scraps. We cleaned it out and on about the third Sunday I was there, we baptized several new converts. Growth was painstakingly slow at first, but we made good use of those altars. I preached as hard as I knew how, and challenged our members week after week to share the gospel. Lo and behold, things began to happen.

I had gone there in February of 1981 and by the end of August when our church year ended, we had baptized 37 people. Our church was growing! The next year we baptized 53 and found ourselves in the midst of a building project. In my third year at

Riverside Baptist Church we decided to have a revival meeting; by this time, there was an air of expectancy when we came to church. Something was happening.

A full time evangelist from Arkansas was our guest preacher for the revival, and on Thursday night he shared his personal testimony of how he had preached as a full-time evangelist for five years averaging 40 meetings a year before realizing that he had never truly been saved. He went to the pastor of the church where he was preaching a revival at the time and told him that God had shown him that he needed to be saved himself, and the pastor led him to Christ and baptized him the very next night. Now, many years later, he was preaching a revival meeting in my first church.

Our church was packed to the gills that night and as the evangelist was preaching, I heard a commotion in the back. As I turned to see what it was, I could see a man who I knew to be a strong leader in another church in the area, a deacon and lay preacher, literally climbing over people to get to the aisle. When he got to the aisle, he ran to the front, slapped his hand on the Communion Table, and said to the preacher, *"Brother, I have known something has been wrong in my heart for years, and tonight God has revealed to me that I have never been truly saved. I need to get saved right now!"* The preacher stopped his sermon, and this man was saved on the spot. We went straight into the invitation and 17 people came forward to be saved. It was glorious! The next night, the air was electrified with the anticipation that God was going to do something great, and another 17 people were saved, including Sunday School teachers, deacons' wives, our church clerk and others! The following Sunday night I baptized 27 people, and to this day that is the most I have ever personally baptized at one time. I didn't know it at the time, but we were experiencing a mighty move of God in revival.

The next year was one of the most exciting years of my entire ministry as our people went out and shared the gospel week after week. People were being saved right and left, and wonderful things were happening in that little church on the backside of town. By the end of that year, we had seen over a hundred people saved, had baptized 95 of them, and had 87 others to join our church by transfer of membership. Out of 2,000 churches in Mississippi we were fifth in baptisms that year.

Someone said to me one day, "You have to go the Mississippi Baptist Convention in November." I said, "Why?" He said, "Because they recognize the top ten churches in baptisms every year, and your church was in the top five!" Not having been raised Baptist, I didn't even know anyone was counting! This was all new to me.

All I knew was that our church had experienced an outpouring of the Spirit of God in revival, and we were excited about telling people about Jesus! Revival had ignited a flame of evangelism in our church. Revival and evangelism go hand in hand.

I know that evangelism is not revival. They are two different things, but I also know that nothing can stir revival fires in a church like seeing people come down the aisle to give their heart to Jesus. We all know that our marching orders have been given. We are to carry the gospel of our Lord to the ends of the earth. But we cannot go further until we go deeper. The church must experience revival in order to fulfill the Great Commission!

Bill McLeod, the pastor in whose church the great Canadian revival was birthed, once said, *"Remember this: In times of evangelism, evangelists seek sinners. But in times of revival, sinners seek the Lord!"*

The preaching of the Gospel was always at the heart of the Great Awakenings. There can be evangelism without revival, but there is no true revival that does not result in evangelism!

When true revival comes—when the Spirit is poured out upon a people—sinners *will* get saved! Revival is for and about the church of the Lord Jesus Christ. No doubt about that. But when the church gets thoroughly right with God and God is alive in them, You will see more people get saved by accident than you could ever see get saved on purpose with an unrevived church. This is true for two reasons: First, because of the "noising about" of what has taken place in the fellowship of believers. Second, because of the extraordinary pouring out of grace upon a repentant and revived people.

In every revival, the fires spread through the power of changed lives. It is well documented that the *fame* of revival spreads the *flame* of revival. Or as someone has well said, *"Revival spreads on the wings of testimonies."*

This is exactly what happened in Acts 4:19-20; 5:38-41, and 17:17 as the people went out in the power of the Holy Spirit, driven by a passionate manifestation of the love of God to share the Gospel. They simply told people what happened to them. And what began as 120 quickly became 3,120 as the Lord added to the church 3,000 souls on the Day of Pentecost. And that 3,120 soon became 5,000 in the city of Jerusalem, and it is estimated that at one time there were as many as 20,000 believers in Jerusalem, with at least one historian saying that number was closer to 50,000. That is the result of revival-driven evangelism!

Whatever else revival is, it is a fresh surrender to Christ that leads His people to a fresh filling of spiritual power as they spontaneously and joyfully share the gospel with the lost. And that is how we fulfill the Great Commission. That has been God's plan all along. No cheap substitutes. No shortcuts. The Great Commission is our marching orders as followers of Christ and can be found at the end of all four gospels and in the first chapter of Acts. The command is for every believer to "go and make disciples" all over the world. The Great Commandment says that we are to love the Lord our God and the Great Commission says that we are to tell the world that God loves them and wants to save them from their sins.

That is a tall order, and that is why we need revival. The church cannot fulfill the Great Commission without being revived.

The Great Shantung Revival of China began when a lady from Norway, Miss Marie Monsen, began asking three questions of Chinese leaders:

1. Have you been born again?

2. What evidence do you have that you have been born again?
3. Have you been filled with the Holy Spirit?

These questions pricked the hearts of those Chinese leaders and they began to seek the Lord in a spirit of repentance, thus birthing one of the greatest revival movements in history. J. Edwin Orr said that between the years 1927 and 1937, this revival affected every province in China. Many call it the "Greatest Revival in Baptist History," although it was not confined to Southern Baptist Churches. It affected dozens of mission agencies and denominations that were working in China at that time. Thousands upon thousands of Chinese people were converted to Christ during this great revival.

One of my favorite people in the world is Dr. Charles Roesel, former pastor of FBC, Leesburg, Florida. He is a living legend in the state of Florida and at 85 years of age is fit and healthy and can still preach the stars down. I had the privilege of hosting him for our 2019 Statewide Senior Adult Evangelism Conference. We had a nice meal in a restaurant before the conference began and shared some wonderful fellowship. Then as we were leaving, he asked the waitress a question. He said, "Do you know for sure that you are saved?" She said, "No sir, I can't say that I do." He said, "Did you know that there are 5 things that will happen to you the moment you get saved?" She said, "No sir, I didn't." He then took about two minutes and shared those five things, and I think it was one of the best presentations of the Gospel I have ever heard:

1. ALL of your sins will be forgiven. *All* of them. Gone forever! (No guilt)
2. All of your sins will be forgotten. (No fear)
3. Jesus Christ will come into your life to enable you to live and to love like you've never lived and loved before. (No weakness)
4. You will become a member of the greatest family on earth —the Family of God. (No loneliness)
5. When you die, you will get to go to Heaven. (No Hell)

I made a mental note of that presentation, and when I got to my room that night, I wrote it down just as he shared it. I used that presentation several times over the next year with great results. One day I was talking with him on the phone, and he began telling me about a gospel presentation he had developed and was in the process of having it printed in a gospel tract. He said it is based on five statements of what happens the moment you get saved. I said, "Let me tell you what those five points are." He seemed surprised that I would know, and I reminded him that I had heard him share it in that restaurant the night I first met him. I gave him the five points and he was pleasantly surprised and very pleased that I could give all five of them.

I like his presentation because it is short, to the point, truthful, and uses the word "saved." I know in our sophisticated, hi-tech world, the word "saved" has lost favor with many, but I think it is still a good word. The Bible uses the word saved a lot, and I don't think we need to get away from it. In Luke 19:10, Jesus says, *"For the Son of Man has come to seek and to **save** that which was lost."* Acts 4:12 says, *"Nor is there salvation in any other, for there is no other name under heaven given among men by which we must be **saved.**"* Romans 10:9 says, *"That if you confess with your mouth the Lord Jesus, and believe in you heart that God has raised Him from the dead, you will be **saved.**"* Ephesians 2:8 says, *"For by grace you have been **saved** through faith, and that not of yourselves, it is the gift of God; not of works, lest anyone should boast.*

We simply cannot afford to become so sophisticated in the church today that we stop talking to people about being "saved."

The greatest message of the church is still, "Jesus saves!" And this is the message the world needs to hear. Believe me when I say this: *There are more people out there who want to hear the Gospel than there are Christians who are willing to share it!*

People are needy! And all the things the world offers them just makes them more needy. They are looking for a solution to their sin, their guilt, their hopelessness and lack of purpose in life. And more often than not, they will welcome a sincere gospel presentation.

I watched this play out recently. I was staying on the top floor of a motel in Prattville, Alabama when an F1 tornado struck the motel and the gas station next to it. The motel received minor damage while the gas station had the roof ripped off of it. We lost electricity, and once I realized that the storm had passed, like many others, I made my way carefully down the dark stairwell to the first floor lobby. We were all standing around sharing stories and grateful to be alive when the Holy Spirit nudged me and God began speaking to my heart. He said, *"Are you going to let this opportunity pass without talking to them about salvation? No one is going anywhere. They're all congregated in groups. They have just had a harrowing experience. Tell them about Me."*

I knew in a moment that I had a great opportunity to share the Gospel. So I walked up to a group of five men and said, "Hey guys, let me ask you a question." They all stopped talking and looked at me. "We've just had a close call. Thank God we're all right. But if that tornado had destroyed this motel, and we would have all died, how many of you are 100% certain you would have gone to heaven?" Three of them didn't respond at all. I learned later that they were Hispanics who didn't speak English. But two others did respond. They were both Romanian. They grew up in the Orthodox Church in Romania, and were now living in Atlanta, Georgia. They were in the area working. We engaged in a wonderful and lively conversation about Jesus and salvation. I was able to share the gospel with them and show that Jesus was the only way to Heaven. They listened intently as I shared with them why religion is not the answer, but Jesus Christ is. When we finished, they both hugged me and thanked me for sharing with them.

I walked over to the other side of the entrance to the motel where another small group of men were talking and listening to some music. I began a similar conversation with them, and when it was over, the most vocal of the group, a tall bearded black men, walked over to me with arms wide open and said, "Man, I want to give you a hug. You have made me think about a lot of things. Thank you. Thank you." When he stepped back, another man stepped in and hugged me, thanking me as well.

No one was saved that night, as far as I can tell, but I went back to my room with joy in my heart because I got to share the gospel with nine people on a night that none of us will ever forget. Seeds were planted, the gospel was given, and now it is up to the Holy Spirit as to what fruit will come from it.

Now, maybe you're thinking, "Brother Terry, you're an evangelism strategist with the Alabama Baptist State Board of Missions. Weren't you disappointed that no one got saved? Did you fail?" Not at all. I still love the old Home Mission Board's definition of successful evangelism: "Successful evangelism is sharing the Gospel in the power of the Holy Spirit and leaving the results up to God." The very first time I ever tried to witness to someone, I was disappointed they didn't get saved. I took it to the Lord, and do you know what He told me? *"That's not your business. That's my business. You are to be a witness. You take care of the witness, and I will take care of the saving."* So, in reality, I was a successful witness, not because someone got saved, but because I was obedient and shared the gospel boldly and compassionately, in the power of the Holy Spirit. The rest is up to God. I went back to my room with "joy unspeakable and full of glory" abounding in my heart.

My point here is that when the gospel is shared, even in a stressful situation, from a sincere and compassionate heart, people will not only listen, but they will receive it gladly, and appreciate it. I will say it again because it has been my experience my entire Christian life: *There are more people out there who want to hear the gospel than there are Christians who are willing to share it."*

Maybe you're reading this and thinking, "Where am I supposed to go to share the gospel?" Let me help you out here. You are asking the wrong question. The question is, "Where *aren't* you supposed to go?" We're supposed to go everywhere! You say, "But what if I witness to the wrong person?" My friend, there is no such thing as witnessing to the wrong person! If we've been told to preach the gospel to every creature as Mark 16:15 commands us, then you cannot possibly witness to the wrong person.

D. L. Moody used to say, "*It is better to tell others about Jesus in a faltering way or even in a mistaken way than not to tell them at all.*" Charles Spurgeon once said, "*Every Christian is either a missionary or an imposter!*"

Having experienced genuine revival, the early church went out in the power of the Holy Spirit and turned the world upside down for Jesus. That's what they said in Thessalonica in Acts 17:6, "*These are they that have turned the world upside down!*"

Somebody said, "They prayed 10 days, preached 10 minutes, and had 3,000 saved! We pray 10 minutes, preach 10 days, and are happy if anyone gets saved!

They experienced revival, and turned the world upside down. Now think about what that actually means. This little rag tag group of believers shook their world for Jesus. And think about the resources that they did *not* have:

No seminaries. No Bible colleges. No gospel television or radio programs. No YouTube sermons. No online Bible courses to take. No Bible conferences. No Sunday School training, or church growth books to read. No missions organizations. No deacon training.

Yet they turned the world upside down for Jesus!

No "how to" clinics. No Christian concerts. No denominations. No Associations. No choirs. No church buildings. No DVD's. No CD's. No Christmas Cantatas. No Easter musicals. No revival meetings. No preaching conferences. No computers. No cell phones. No billboards. No copiers. No Gospel tracts. No posters or flyers. No automobiles, no planes, no trains. No UPS or postal service. No Adrian Rogers, or Charles Stanley, or David Jeremiah to listen to.

Yet they turned the world upside down for Jesus!

They had no beautiful sanctuaries. No mega churches. No carpet. No VBS. No air conditioning. No comfortable pews. No nurseries.

No such thing as a Bible in every hand. They didn't even have a New Testament yet!

Yet they turned the world upside down for Jesus!

How did they do it? They simply experienced the power of the Holy Spirit falling on Pentecost and they went out in the power of the Spirit and shared the glorious gospel of Jesus Christ. It worked then and it still works today. But we have to have the fire of the Holy Spirit!

The secret to the power of the early church was not in what they had or what they knew, or what they could do, but in the fact that they stayed in the upper room just as Christ commanded them to do until they were endued with power from on high. That being said, I think I know what our problem is today. We have left the upper room too soon! We have not waited before God in humility and total dependence upon Him. We have forgotten that *"It is not by might, nor by strength, but my Spirit," says the Lord of Hosts."* (Zechariah 4:6)

There was a difference of epic proportions between the disciples *before* the Spirit fell and the disciples *after* the Spirit fell:

Before the Spirit fell, they were **Apprehensive**. After the Spirit fell they were **Alert**.

Before the Spirit fell, they were **Bland**. After the Spirit fell they were **Bold**.

Before the Spirit fell, they were **Complacent**. After the Spirit fell they were **Crusaders**.

Before the Spirit fell, they were **Dejected & Discouraged**. After the Spirit fell they were **Devoted & Dynamic**.

Before the Spirit fell, they were **Empty**. After the Spirit fell they were **Empowered**.

Before the Spirit fell, they were **Fearful & Fickle**. After the Spirit fell they were **Filled, Focused, and on Fire**.

Before the Spirit fell, they were **Gloomy & Gullible**. After the Spirit fell they were **Gallant & Gung-Ho**.

Before the Spirit fell, they were **Hiding**. After the Spirit fell they were **Heroes**.

Before the Spirit fell, they were **Immature**. After the Spirit fell they were **Imitators**.

Before the Spirit fell, they were **Jittery**. After the Spirit fell they were **Joyful**.

Before the Spirit fell, they were **Kittens**. After the Spirit fell they were **Kings**.

Before the Spirit fell, they were **Lazy**. After the Spirit fell they were **Lions**.

Before the Spirit fell, they were **Mediocre**. After the Spirit fell they were **Mighty**.

Before the Spirit fell, they were **Negligent**. After the Spirit fell they were **Noble**.

Before the Spirit fell, they were **Opinionated**. After the Spirit fell they were **Obedient**.

Before the Spirit fell, they were **Passive & Pathetic**. After the Spirit fell they were **Powerful**.

Before the Spirit fell, they were **Quarrelsome**. After the Spirit fell they were **Qualified**.

Before the Spirit fell, they were **Reluctant**. After the Spirit fell they were **Ready & Renewed**.

Before the Spirit fell, they were **Silent**. After the Spirit fell they were **Soldiers**.

Before the Spirit fell, they were **Timid**. After the Spirit fell they were **Transformed**.

Before the Spirit fell, they were **Unstable**. After the Spirit fell they were **Unified & Unafraid**.

Before the Spirit fell, they were **Victims**. After the Spirit fell they were **Victors**.

Before the Spirit fell, they were **Wimps**. After the Spirit fell they were **Warriors**.

Before the Spirit fell, they were **Yellow**. After the Spirit fell they were **Yielded**.

Before the Spirit fell, they were **Zeroes**. After the Spirit fell they were **Zealous**.

The revival that came on Pentecost catapulted the first century church into the world with the gospel message fresh on their minds and the name of Jesus on their tongues, and the world has never been the same since. Oh! How we need that again!

I believe that the average Christian and the average church are bogged down somewhere between Calvary and Pentecost. They made it to Calvary for pardon, but stopped short of Pentecost for power.

Bethlehem means God *with* us!

Calvary means God *for* us!

But Pentecost boldly declares that God is *in* us to empower us to serve the Lord Jesus Christ!

God, the Father is God *without skin*, God the Son is God *with skin*, but God the Holy Spirit is God *in our skin!*

God the Father is the only God you will ever *know*.

God the Son is the only God you will ever *see*.

But God, the Holy Spirit is the only God you will ever *feel!*

. . .

What I'm trying to say is the Holy Spirit is our power and without Him, we have no hope of winning our world to Christ and seeing a mighty revival sweep across our barren land.

Dr. Stephen Olford, one of the greatest preachers of the nineteenth century used to say,

> *"If the sin of the Old Testament was a rejection of God the Father, and the sin of the New Testament was a rejection of God the Son, then the sin of our day is the rejection of God, the Holy Spirit!"*

There is a well-worn story of how an old deacon got carried away and mixed up his metaphors. He prayed, "Lord, if any spark of awakening has been lit in this revival meeting, we pray that you will water that spark!" And after we wipe the smile from our faces, we should be compelled to ask, "Who watered the spark?"

When did we lose our burning passion to tell people about Jesus? We need men and women who are on fire proclaiming truth with passion, calling for a deep, heartfelt surrender to Jesus. That is the crying need of this hour.

In Mark 16:15 Jesus commanded us to *"Go into all the world and preach the gospel to every creature."* He didn't stutter. He didn't stammer. And He didn't put it in the form of a suggestion. It is a command. It is our mission!

Evangelist and author Ray Comfort sheds some insightful humor on this verse:

> *"And by the way, here is a fascinating thing about that verse. The original Greek meaning of "Go into all the world and preach the gospel to every creature" opens up some interesting thoughts. The word for "go" in the Greek is poreuomai, meaning "go." The word for "all" also carries with it gripping connotations. It is the word hapas and it means literally "every." It is pas, and it means literally "every." So when Jesus said, "God into all the world and*

preach the gospel to every creature" to be true and faithful to the Greek text, what He was actually saying was, "Go into all the world and preach the gospel to every creature." It's amazing what insights the Greek can give you!"

Someone has said that we should have the head of a Baptist, the heart of a Pentecostal, and the feet of a Jehovah's Witness. That would be a winning combination, in my opinion!

I have actually heard people say, "I would witness, but I don't feel called. That's just not my gift." I want to say to them, *"What part of the word 'Go' do you not understand?"* Sure, there are those who have the gift of Evangelism. They have a unique, God-given ability to share the gospel and see people saved on a regular basis. I praise God for them! But that does not negate the fact that we are *all* called to share the gospel. You cannot use the "I don't have the gift" excuse to not share the good news that Jesus saves! You cannot say, "I just don't feel qualified to share the gospel."

One day many years ago an old blind man made his way to the compound of the China Inland Mission. Patiently and skillfully, the hospital staff removed cataracts from his eyes. The old gentleman was so happy with the miracle of sight. Now he was able to see! He moved about the hospital grounds sharing his joy with all who would listen.

One day the hospital staff missed him and searched the compound thoroughly, but he was not to be found. Three days later, they saw this old man walking up the road toward the compound. He was holding to the end of a long rope and attached to the rope was a dozen men. The joyful old man had walked back to his province and looked up every blind person he could find and was leading them to the place and the persons who gave him his sight.

And isn't that what we should be doing? Out of a heart of joy and gratefulness for all God has done for us, shouldn't we be bringing others to Christ, no matter what our problems or limitations are?

It's true that we cannot do everything, but all of us can say this: "I cannot do everything, but I can do something. And by the grace of

God, I will do that something that I can do, and give God all the glory!

George Stott, the 19th Century missionary to China, served faithfully despite having only one leg. When asked why he, with only one leg, should think of going to China, his reply was, "I do not see those with two legs going, so I must." May his tribe increase!

If you were able to discover the cure for cancer, would you be justified in keeping it to yourself because you are shy, or nervous about speaking to others? Wouldn't it be criminal to not tell those who are dying of cancer that you have the cure? We have the cure for a malady that is much worse than cancer. It's called sin! And here's the tragic part. Sin carries with it a 100% fatality. *"The wages of sin is death."* (Romans 6:23) The last time I checked, 10 out of 10 people die. And the Bible teaches that those who die without Jesus Christ spend an eternity in Hell. So sin is a much worse "disease" than cancer. And the cure for sin is the gospel of Jesus Christ. If you are a Christian, you have the cure! So the question is, "What are you doing with it?"

I heard about a man who was an unbeliever who found out that his friend of 20 years was a Christian. He never knew it. His friend had never mentioned his Christian faith to him. This man accused his friend of being a hypocrite, and declared that his faith was bogus. The friend was shocked. "Why would you say that about my faith?" he asked. "Because if you *really* believed what you say you believe, then every person who doesn't know Christ is going to die and go to Hell. Yet you have known me for 20 years, and have never even mentioned Christ to me. If I believed what you claim to believe, I would crawl a hundred miles over broken glass to warn my friends about Hell. I would not let *anything* stop me from telling my friends about Jesus Christ! Yet you have never once talked to me about Jesus."

> A hundred thousand souls a day
> Are passing one by one away
> In Christless guilt and gloom;

> O Church of Christ, what wilt thou say
> When on that awful judgment day
> They charge THEE with their doom!

There are roughly 7 billion people in the world today and the best estimates are that only 1/3 of the population of the world profess to be Christian. That number includes all who identify themselves as Christians, whether religiously, socially, or politically. Many in that number are not actually followers of Jesus Christ. But if we were to to assume they all were, that still leaves about 4.5 billion people who, if the gospel is true at all, are at this moment separated from God in their sin and if nothing changes will spend an eternity in Hell. Again, that is 4.5 billion people. One heartbeat from Hell.

Now that is a big number. Do you know how long it would take to count to just 1 billion if you counted at the rate of one number per second? I have asked that question to groups many times over the last several years and the answers range from "several days," to "one week," to "about a month." But, at one number per second, it would actually take you 37 years to count to one billion. 37 years! And that's just to 1 billion. There are 4.5 billion people on planet earth right now who are without Christ. That is a staggering thought that should put us on our knees.

Or to put it another way: What is 750,000 miles long, would wrap around the earth 31 times, and grows 20 miles longer every single day? Answer: The line of unsaved people alive on earth today. Wow!

And here's the amazing thing: God knows every one of those people by name. He created every single one of them. He fashioned them in their mother's womb, watched them as they took their first step, knows every hair on their head and loves them with a perfect love. He wants more than anything to have a relationship with them and He wants them to come to Heaven and spend eternity with Him in the place He has prepared for them. And yet, if nothing changes, those 4.5 billion people will die in their sins never having accepted Jesus Christ, God's Son, as their Lord and Savior. And they will go to Hell.

That is why Paul talks about in Romans 1:14-15 being a debtor to all the nations. A debtor! Paul says he owes a debt to every lost person on the face of the planet. Because he is owned by Jesus, he owes Jesus to the world. According to the Apostle Paul, *every saved person this side of Heaven owes the gospel to every lost person this side of Hell!* We owe Christ to the world!

> From the least to the greatest!
>
> From the poorest to the richest!
>
> From the most ignorant to the most educated!
>
> From the people here at home to those around the world.
>
> We are debtors with the gospel to the whole world!

And do you know why? I want you to hear it again as if you're hearing it for the very first time:

> *"For God so loved the world, that He gave His only begotten Son, that whosoever believeth in Him should not perish, but have everlasting life." --* John 3:16

That's why we go. Because God loves the world and tells us to go and share the gospel with them. Charles Spurgeon said,

> *"Brethren, do something, do something, do something! While societies and unions make constitutions, let us win souls. I pray you, be men of action all of you. Get to the work and quit yourselves like men. Old Suvarov's idea of war is mine: "forward and strike! No theory! Attack! Form a column! Charge bayonets! Plunge into the center of the enemy! Our one aim is to win souls; and this we are not to talk about, but do in the power of God!"*

Back when I was in seminary, a professor one day criticized one of my classmates for using the phrase "winning souls." He said, "We ought not talk about "winning" souls, like it is a ballgame we're playing. We don't "win" souls, we share the gospel. We give witness to our faith. We spread the gospel. But we shouldn't talk about "winning souls." I thought that sounded erudite and sophisticated, so I stopped using the phrase. Until one day I came across I Corinthians 9: 19-22 where Paul refers to winning souls six times in four verses:

> *"For though I am free from all men, I have made myself a servant to all, that I might **win** the more; and to the Jews I became as a Jew, that I might **win** Jews; to those who are under the law, as under the law, that I might **win** those who are under the law; to those who are without the law, as without the law (not being without law toward God, but under law toward Christ), that I might **win** those who are without law; to the weak I became weak, that I might **win** the weak. I have become all things to all men, that I might by all means **save** some.*

"Soul winning" is a biblical concept. Winning souls is the business of the Church! If Paul can talk about it in those terms, then so can we! D.L. Moody asked a man about the condition of his soul one day, and the man said, "Sir, I would appreciate it if you would mind your own business." To which Moody replied, "*Sir, winning souls to Christ is my business.*" Andrew Murray said, "*There are two kinds of Christians: Soul winners and backsliders. God could have chosen angels, but He didn't. He chose you.*"

God had only one Son, and He made Him a soul winner. The ministry of Jesus Christ was one of personal soul winning. Everywhere He went He won people, personally.

> He won a religious leader, Nicodemas, personally.
>
> He won the woman caught in the act of adultery, personally.
>
> He won the woman at the well, personally.
>
> He won a demon-possessed person, personally.
>
> He won Bartimaeus, a blind beggar, personally.
>
> He won Mary Magdalene, personally.

> He won Zacchaeus, a cheat, personally.
>
> He won Matthew, a tax collector, personally.
>
> Everywhere he went, He won people, personally.
>
> If I claim to be a follower of Jesus Christ, I will also seek to win souls to Him.

So here are two very important questions: First, "When was the last time you won someone to Christ, personally?" And maybe more importantly, "When was the last time you tried?"

In a revival service many years ago, I sank down in my seat under deep conviction when the evangelist asked those two questions just like that. I knew there was so much more I could be doing to win souls to Jesus.

But we're not winning our world to Jesus. The population is growing while the church is shrinking. Salvations and baptisms are at an all time low. What is the problem! I'll tell you what I think it is: We are majoring on minors, and minoring on the majors. We've gotten our priorities all mixed up and we're chasing fleas and having our "teas" while the drug dealers, pornographers, race baiters and the woke mob are devouring our land and destroying our children! While we're having our parties and programs, the world is marching into Hell fire because the church has lost its revival fires! Brethren, it is time for the church to wake up! We must repent of preaching a dynamite gospel and living firecracker lives!

We must fall on our faces in repentance, ask God to fill us once again with the Holy Spirit and then go tell a lost and dying world about a Savior who is alive and can save them from their sins and change their lives forever!

Sometimes people ask me if we Baptists believe every Christian should be filled with the Holy Spirit. I love to answer that question this way: I believe every Christian should be so filled with the Holy Spirit that if a mosquito bites him, he flies away singing, "There's power in the blood!"

And if there's one thing I know about being filled with the Holy Spirit, it is this: whatever else you may or may not do when you are filled with the Spirit, you *will* speak the Word of God with boldness. *"...and they were all filled with the Holy Spirit, and they spoke the Word of God with boldness."* (Acts 4:31b)

C.T. Studd, a man of unbelievable spiritual power said, *"Some wish to live within the sound of a church and chapel bell, but I want to run a rescue shop within a yard of Hell!"*

My dear friend, the bottom line is if we go, they will come. And if we don't go, they simply will not come. We must go. The word "go" is found 255 times in Scripture and Jesus was constantly telling people to "go."

Go tell. Go and sin no more. Go in peace. Go preach. Go into the street. Go wash in the pool of Siloam. Go show yourself to the priest. Go, your faith has made you whole. Go and make disciples. Go make it right with your brother. Go quickly.

> You cannot spell God without spelling go.
>
> You cannot spell good without spelling go.
>
> You cannot spell Gospel without spelling go.
>
> Will you go?

A good two-part sermon is this: Go and Sat. God wants you to "go." Satan wants you to "Sat." We must go. But we must go in love! We must go in His Spirit! We must go in His name! But, at whatever cost, we must go!

> We must go before it is too late!
>
> We must go with faith!
>
> We must go with the authority of Jesus Christ!

We must go in the name of the King of Kings and the Lord of Lords!

We must go with the love of Jesus pounding in our heart!

We must go because Hell is hot, heaven is sweet, life is short, eternity is long, death is certain, and God is worth it all!

Will you go?

All of us must go.

Each of us must go.

Every one of us must go.

The fields are ripe unto harvest!

We are in a race against time, against sin, and against death.

We have no time to waste and no time to lose.

We must go and keep on going until every person we can possibly reach knows that Jesus died on the cross for them!

Will you go?

Will you let revival spring up in your heart, and then go forth and tell a lost world that Jesus still saves!

> "Could a lifeguard sit idle, if he heard a drowning cry?
> Could a doctor sit in comfort, and let his patient die?
> Could a fireman sit and watch men burn and offer no hand?
> Can we sit at ease in Zion, with the world around us damned?

My dear friend, I have but one question as I close this chapter.

Will you go?

13

CHARACTERISTIC # 10 AWAKENING

A SIGNIFICANT IMPACT UPON THE COMMUNITY AT LARGE

The last great revival in Western Civilization, unless you count the Jesus Revival of the 1970's, was the Welsh Revival of 1904-05. It began in prayer. A Presbyterian preacher by the name of Seth Joshua prayed in a meeting, *"O God, bend us!"*

A young coal miner turned seminary student, Evan Roberts, was in the crowd that night. He went to his room and prayed, *"O God, bend ME!"* From the depths of God's dealing with his heart, he began leading prayer meetings with young people, putting forth his four keys to revival:

1. You must confess any known sin to God and put any wrong done to others right.
2. You must put away any doubtful habit.
3. You must obey the Spirit promptly.
4. You must confess your faith in Christ publicly.

The result of his preaching in Wales was undeniable. Scores of people were saved. It is reported that 100,000 souls were saved in 9 months in Wales. Whole towns and villages were caught up in revival. The names of those saved were listed in the newspapers. There was such a drop in crime that police officers formed quartets because there were virtually no crimes to process. There were no reported rapes, burglaries, or murders. It is said that the mules in the mines had to be retrained because their owners had stopped cursing and the mules didn't recognize their voice! Even the mules knew it when revival came!

Author Dave Keesling said it this way: *"The Gospel's simplicity is its ability to, in a single moment, change literally everything."*

A.W. Tozer echoed this belief in an article he entitled *"There is no Limit to Revival":*

> *"There is no limit to what God could do in our world if we would dare to surrender before Him with a commitment that says, "Oh God, I hereby give myself to You. I give my family. I give my business. I give all I possess. Take all of it, Lord—and take me! I give myself in such measure that if it is necessary that I lose everything for Your sake, let me lose it. I will not ask what the price is. I will ask only that I may be all that I ought to be as a follower and disciple of Jesus Christ."*
>
> *If even 300 of God's people became that serious, our world would never hear the last of it! They would influence the news. Their message would go everywhere like birds on the wing. They would set off a great revival on New Testament faith and witness. God wants to deliver us from the easygoing, smooth and silky, fat and comfortable Christianity so fashionable today."*

It is true that there is absolutely no limit to what God can do in revival, but we must acknowledge that only God can do it. We do not have the power to fix our hearts, our homes, our churches and our nation, but God is waiting for us to turn to Him and ask Him to do it. Author and Pastor Ray Ortlund, Jr. says,

"When God rends the heavens and comes down on His people, a divine power achieves what human effort at its best fails to do. God's people thirst for the ministry of the Word and receive it with tender meltings of soul. The grip of the enslaving sin is broken. Reconciliation between believers is sought and granted. Spiritual things, rather than material things, capture people's hearts. A defensive, timid church is transformed into a confident army. Believers joyfully suffer for their Lord. They treasure usefulness to God over career advancement. Communion with God is avidly enjoyed. Churches and Christian organizations reform their policies and procedures. People who had always been indifferent to the Gospel now inquire anxiously. And this type of spiritual movement draws in not just the isolated straggler here and there but large numbers of people. A wave of divine grace washes over the church and spills out onto the world. That is what happens when God comes down. And that is how we should pray for the church today."

This kind of vision for revival should bring us back to prayer again and again begging and pleading with God to send "a wave of divine grace to wash over the church and spill out onto the world."

Such was the case with the Welsh Revival of 1904. In "The Nature of God-Sent Revival," Duncan Campbell said,

> *"The difference in successful evangelism, and revival, is this: In evangelism, the two, the three, the ten, the twenty, and possibly the hundred make confessions of Jesus Christ, and at the end of the year you are thankful if half of them are still standing. But the community remains untouched. The public houses are crowded, the dancing ballrooms, packed. The theatre and the picture houses are patronized by the hundreds. No change in the community.*
>
> *But in revival, when God, the Holy Ghost comes; when the winds of heaven blow suddenly, the whole community becomes God-conscious! A God-realization takes hold of young, middle-aged, and old. So that, as in the case of the Hebrides Revival, 75% of those saved one night were saved before they came near a meeting!"*

Speaking of the Island of Berneray, he said,

> *"I question if there was one single house on the island that wasn't visited that night! An awareness of God, a consciousness of God, seemed to hover over the very atmosphere! The very atmosphere seemed to be charged with the power of Almighty God! That is revival!"*

You may be thinking, "That happened a long time ago. Can that kind of thing really happen today? ? In an issue of *Spirit of Revival* Magazine, published by Life Action Ministries, I read a thrilling account of a woman whose life had been impacted by a revival meeting in her church. She said,

> *"First, I quit smoking after forty-three years, using no man-made helps—the power of prayer works. Second (and most important), was my son's salvation. He was saved last month and baptized on Easter Sunday. I can't tell you the joy I felt after nineteen years of prayers and tears to see that answer come."*

But that was just the beginning. Over a short period of time following the revival that began in her own heart, this happened:

> *"My brother-in-law was saved, my mother was saved, my niece was saved, my nephew and his wife rededicated their lives to Christ, my daughter rededicated her life, my daughter's fiancé was saved, my daughter's friend was saved, my granddaughter was baptized, my husband is growing spiritually, my daughter's fiance's sister was saved, and my son's fiance's daughter was saved."*

This is what can happen when the fire falls and one person experiences genuine revival. As I said before, you will see more people saved by accident with revival than you could ever see saved on purpose without it!

Here is one account of how even a pastor's life was changed by the power of revival. It is rather lengthy, but, realizing that the "fame of revival spreads on the flames of testimony," I have included it in total in hopes that God may stir your heart just from reading it as He did mine when I first read it:

WHEN THE FIRE FALLS

"Several weeks ago, God broke into our services in an amazing way. It is almost too sacred to mention and amazing to tell for fear of stealing credit or robbing God.

After returning from a revival conference, and the night before I was to lead Sunday services at my church, I read the biography of Manley Beasley and was completely torn inside and challenged greatly in the area of devotion, prayer, and faith. Broken over what I knew God was showing me about myself, I watched a sermon on "The Fear of Man" around 4:00 a.m. in the morning. Completely devastated, I knew what God was leading me to do.

I threw away my sermon notes for what I had planned to preach, and went to Jeremiah 2:13. Instead, I preached about my sin of pride. I confessed my insecurity rooted in pride. I opened up about attempting to be a people-pleaser and attempting to hold water in broken cisterns. No outline, not a fancy sermon. I was just broken before my people and honest about God's desire for revival in our church.

At the invitation I beheld a glimpse of God's glory. About 90 percent of our church found a place at the altar. No music, no time limits—just people crying out for revival. After people were done praying, we sat in silence in awe of the presence of God. It was sacred and I dared not to say a thing. We sat, we prayed, we cried, God was real.

Since that time, the Holy Spirit has continued to move. We have had similar invitations every week. Church has become so much more than the music, the preaching, or even the people. **It has become a symphony of people crying out for God to move.** *Our prayer meetings are intense. Faith is growing for what only God can do. People are being saved and transformed by the gospel. Men, women, and teens are praying.*

I said all of that to say what God has placed in my heart is a deep burden for revival. I cannot drive to a single church, in a single town, in any state and not wonder what God is doing there, and what could God do if His people sought His glorious presence? What would happen if He sent revival? What would happen if God would do something that could not be explained by anything else than Him?

Every town, big or small, I wonder and I pray. I go through Wal-Mart and wonder what could God do. I feel despair that the majority of these people do not know Christ, and unless we see a mighty move of God, they may never come to Christ. I pray earnestly for God to rend the heavens and come down. This burden has intensified to an inferno in my soul. I wake up with it and go to sleep with it. "Lord, bend me!"

This is just a glimpse of what God can do in a church when genuine revival comes! Wouldn't you love for your church to be a "symphony of people crying out to God" for revival?

I will close this book by sharing a story from history that forms the backdrop for a special invitation I sometimes give in revival meetings. I pray this will challenge you to "step across the line" to see God move in your church in genuine revival.

In March of 1836, the people of Texas decided they would no longer be in bondage to the Mexican government and would fight for their independence. After 21 days of fighting, 183 Texans made a last ditch stand at a Spanish Mission in San Antonio, called The Alamo. Among the men there were Colonel William Travis, Steven F. Austin, Davy Crockett, and Jim Bowie.

The odds were not in their favor. The Mexican army, under the command of General Santa Anna, numbering from between 3,000 and 5,000 had completely surrounded the Alamo. Santa Anna issued a challenge: *"Put down your guns, surrender, and promise never to take up weapons against Mexico again, and your lives will be spared."*

On the inside, Colonel Travis was in charge. He told the men that there was no way he was going to surrender. He said, *"If you stay you will likely die. If you want to go home, you can go now."* One French mercenary named Moses Rose went over the wall and later told the story. Travis took his saber, drew a line in the sand, and told the men, "If you want to fight, step across the line." To the man, they all stepped across the line, except for Bowie, who was wounded and was lying on a cot. He said, *"Don't leave me! I may be wounded, but drag me across the line and I'll fight."*

Colonel Travis stepped to the rampart and shouted, *"Sir, we will not surrender, nor retreat! Long live the Republic of Texas!"* And then he fired a cannon shot at the enemy.

Santa Anna issued a charge, and the Texans were summarily slaughtered. Santa Anna thought that was the end, celebrated the victory, and took his weary troops to San Jacinto to rest.

Nineteen days later, The Mexican troops were camped near San Jacinto when a certain General by the name of Sam Houston, from the state of Tennessee, and his 600 troops surrounded them and caught them by surprise. Santa Anna was asleep under an old Cottonwood tree when he heard the click of a rifle hammer. When he opened his eyes he was looking up the barrel of an old 50 caliber Sharp Buffalo rifle, aimed right between his eyes. In a slow Tennessee drawl, Sam Houston said, *"Sir, surrender. Remember the Alamo!"*

Now, I want you to imagine a line being drawn in the sand with the Civil War replica saber that I bought just for the purpose of giving this specific invitation. When I am in a church service, I draw the saber, walk down to the floor and with the point of the sword, I draw an imaginary line all the way across the front of the sanctuary. I then ask the people who feel desperate for revival, and are willing to lay it all down in surrender to the Lordship of Christ, to walk forward and step across the line. I ask the pastor and staff to come first. Once they are on the other side of the line, I then invite all those who will stand with them to come forward and "step across the line" indicating their total commitment to the cause of Christ, the cause of lost souls, and the cause of revival, in that community. More often than not, almost the entire church comes forward.

So now, dear reader, I would like to ask you a most important question. Are you willing to "step across the line" and lay it all down for the possibility of revival in the church, and for spiritual awakening in our nation? Would you make a commitment to pray for revival until it comes? Would you say to Satan and all the demons of Hell, "I will not surrender, nor retreat! Remember

Calvary! Long live the cause of Christ! Long live the blood-bought church of the Lord Jesus Christ!"

Would you join me and tens of thousands of others around the nation in praying for an outpouring of the Spirit in genuine revival and spiritual awakening, so that Christ is glorified, souls are saved, the church is transformed, and America returns to God?

May God help us to do it. And may we once again see the Fire of Heaven fall!

Beloved reader, this book has been an expression of my heart cry for revival in our churches and in our land. Like thousands of others, I have a burden to see genuine revival in my lifetime. This burden is what led me to spend 100 days at a roadside cross praying for revival in my home county in south Mississippi in 2012. That life-changing experience is documented in my first book published in 2020 entitled, *100 Days at the Cross*. I am constantly amazed at how God is using that book and the testimony of what He accomplished at that roadside cross.

If you would like to purchase a copy of *100 Days at the Cross*, you can contact me at 205-245-4286, or email me at Tlong@alsbom.org. Or you can simply go to Amazon and order it from there. If your life has been challenged, or blessed, or if you have given your heart to Jesus Christ as a result of either of these two books, or know someone that has, I would love to know about it. Thank you for taking time to read my book.

May we together experience the glory of God when the fire of the Holy Spirit falls upon us in genuine revival!

If you were blessed by this book, please consider posting a review on Amazon.com. That will help others discover the book.

ABOUT THE AUTHOR

After pastoring Southern Baptist churches for 40 years, Terry Long became an Associational Missions Director for Choctaw County Baptist Association in Butler, Alabama in 2015 where he presently resides. In addition to that, he also serves part time in the Evangelism Office of the Alabama Baptist State Board of Missions as a Spiritual Renewal and Revival Strategist. Dr. Long is a graduate of William Carey University, New Orleans Baptist

Theological Seminary, and the Southern Baptist Center for Biblical Studies. He has been married to his wife, Judy, for 43 years, and together, they have four children and nine grandchildren. His first book, *100 Days at the Cross*, won the 2020 Notable Book award by the Southern Christian Writers Conference.

ALSO BY TERRY LONG

100 Days at the Cross - One man's journey to understanding the Power of the Cross of Christ

Available from the author or at Amazon.com

Made in the USA
Columbia, SC
22 October 2021